Selecting Effective Pastoral Staff

How to Find the Right Fit for Your Church

Wil M. Spaite

Foreword by Jim L. Bond

Beacon Hill Press of Kansas City
Kansas City, Missouri

Library of Congress Cataloging-in-Publication-Data

Spaite, Wil M., 1931-
  Selecting effective pastoral staff : how to find the right fit for your church / Wil M. Spaite.
    p. cm.
  Includes bibliographical references.
  ISBN 0-8341-2101-8 (pbk.)
  1. Church of the Nazarene—Clergy—Appointment, call, and election. 2. Church officers—Selection and appointment. I. Title.

  BX8699.N35.S63 2004
  254—dc22

                                                                    2004001453

10 9 8 7 6 5 4 3 2 1

To Pollie, my wonderful wife,
a woman of prayer and a true partner in our ministry.
To our children—Dave, Dan, and Judi—
who are all followers of Jesus and are a blessing to our world.
And to district superintendents, pastors, staff, and lay leaders
whose friendship has enriched our lives.

Contents

Foreword

A surging, almost urgent, interest in the subject of leadership has taken place in recent years. Books on leadership have proliferated in the market. Educational institutions have created new courses, departments, and delivery systems. The business and corporate world has poured millions of dollars into forums and seminars to enhance the skills of their managers. All of this has raised our understanding and practicing of leadership to new levels.

Why this penchant for leadership? Because it is critical to the success of any entity, be it the home, school, corporation, nation, or church. Organizations must have focus, inspiration, and direction from those in charge. Without it they languish; with it they can potentially flourish.

I travel throughout the world, getting an up-close-and-personal view of the Church. At all echelons of the Church it is quite apparent that success turns on the quality of its leadership. It may come from the superintendent of a district or the senior pastor of a local church, both of whom are bringing forth the best from themselves and others. It may emanate from pastoral staff members or laypeople exercising leadership giftedness. Regardless of who functions as leader, if the Church is to maximize its ministry effectiveness, we must liberate the leadership potential in everyone, clergy and laity alike. This is imperative if the Church is to be God's place for realized human potential.

This book, authored by Wil Spaite, is unique amid the plethora of material on leadership in the church. It is founded on the principle that the selection of an individual for a specific leadership role is virtually as important as the skills he or she may possess for the assignment. Functioning in a position for which one is not well suited is asking anyone less than a David to don Saul's armor for battle. Thus, the sometimes onerous but ultimately fulfilling task of senior leadership is to match the gifts and graces of individuals with the specific needs of the organization. This book focuses particularly on a couple of issues: the district superintendent's responsibility in assisting a local church in the calling of a senior pastor, and the senior pastor's role in the hiring of staff and engagement of laypeople for positions of service in the church.

There is no guarantee of a perfect fit every time when attempting to match individuals to positions. Regardless, if we expect leaders at the various levels of the church to accomplish their objectives, they must be provided the right tools—and the right people in the right assignments are the most important tools a leader can have. This is why the selection process is of paramount importance.

Church polity and structural procedures in each denomination provide guidance in the calling of people to leadership roles. Corporate models for decision making may also prove beneficial. Obviously, the biblical principle of discerning direction through the guidance of the One who is the Head of the Church is crucial in our choices. The value of Dr. Spaite's book is that it pragmatizes the process, giving sound and practical directives to decision makers. This is a logistical how-to book for the selection of leaders in the church.

I know of no one better equipped to write such a sensible, beneficial book as my cherished friend and highly regarded colleague of many years, Wil Spaite. He has distinguished himself at all levels of his denomination—general, regional university, district, local—as a proven, perceptive, and productive leader. Of particular importance in the writing of this book, Dr. Spaite served effectively as senior pastor with multiple staff and as a district superintendent with oversight of 60 churches. During his 20 years as superintendent, the Central California District thrived, including the doubling of morning worship attendance. The average length of tenure for pastors in the Church of the Nazarene is 3.3 years. Under Dr. Spaite's leadership, his pastors served an average of 6.5 years per pastorate. He attributes a measure of the success of his district to the longer tenure of his pastors. Further, he believes that the longer pastorates are directly related to the high priority he assigned to the process of ensuring a good fit of pastor and church. He was intent on getting the right person in the right assignment.

Out of his rich and varied experiences in selecting persons for leadership in the church, Dr. Spaite now shares his accrued knowledge. To read, study, and utilize these resources will greatly enhance the process of leadership selection in the church, which is essential to more effective mission accomplishment.

—Jim L. Bond
General Superintendent
Church of the Nazarene

Acknowledgments

The idea of writing a book was not a one-time revelation. It developed gradually. I think it started when staff members and newly assigned pastors expressed gratitude to me for the process that led to the confirmation of their calls.

My wife, Pollie, encouraged me to put my thoughts into writing, even though she knew it would mean sacrificing some of our treasured time together. Across the years she has shared my interest in finding the "right" leaders. Before every staff or pastoral interview, she was there with me to meet the candidate and his or her spouse. She has an amazing ability to discern the attitudes of prospects and spouses.

My friend Jesse Middendorf, former fellow district superintendent and pastor and now general superintendent, had a part in my deciding to proceed. I discussed with him the need for a book on choosing leaders. The next day he sought me out and said, "You need to do it!"

Jim Bond's offering to write the foreword also encouraged me to continue the project. He has been a lifelong friend with whom I've had the privilege of being a partner in ministry. I have great confidence in his wise and candid approach to leadership as a pastor, college president, and general superintendent.

Special thanks go to the senior pastors who have contributed what they look for in staff members and how they lead their congregations in welcoming new staff: Mark Fuller, Larry Leonard, Mel McCullough, Tim Stearman, and J. K. Warrick. I also thank my district superintendent, Daniel Copp, for the sample bonding service in the appendix.

This book would not have been possible without the typing of the manuscript by Retha Cook—one of our office secretaries here at Oro Valley Church. Her patient and capable work beyond her office hours was an inspiration to me.

Beacon Hill Press of Kansas City director Bonnie Perry was a positive help in recognizing the need for such a book. Her suggestions on preparing the manuscript for the Book Committee are appreciated.

Finally, I want to express my gratitude to my present senior pastor, Craig Coulter, for his ongoing support in the writing of this book. My associate ministry here in teaming with him and the other pastoral staff has been a delight.

Introduction
The Adventure of Calling Leaders

Much has been written on the important subject of leadership. But an area often overlooked is how to select the right leaders.

This book is for those responsible for choosing leaders to serve in local churches. It is written for—

- Senior pastors who are considering the hiring of pastoral staff.
- Pastoral staff members who are interested in identifying and developing the qualities desired by senior pastors.
- District/Conference leaders who recommend pastoral candidates.
- Assistants appointed by a district/conference leader to preside in calling pastors.

I have discovered across the years that *choosing leaders wisely is a challenging adventure—an adventure that will have a far-reaching impact on the eternal destiny of lives.* If you stop to consider the results from well-placed or misplaced leaders, you will become keenly aware of the real growth or dismal decline of Christian churches.

In the world of business leadership, Jim Collins has published a recent best-selling book, *Good to Great.* Collins and his research team studied corporations in America and identified 11 companies that have sustained major growth over the past 15 years. One of the first principles that became evident in all 11 "great" corporations is

FIRST WHO . . . THEN WHAT. We expected that good-to-great leaders would begin by setting a new vision and strategy. We found instead that they *first* got the right people on the bus, the wrong people off the bus, and the right people in the right seats—and *then* they figured out where to drive it. The old adage "people are your most important asset" turns out to be wrong. People are *not* your most important asset. The *right* people are![1]

Whenever you find a great church, it will be led by a pastor who is an effective preacher of the Word and also has learned to make wise choices of staff and lay leaders.

When I was a senior pastor and later a district superintendent, I would have welcomed information on how to *choose* the *right* staff and senior pastors. The purpose of this book is to address the question "How can I become more effective in selecting the right persons for leadership positions?" I have discovered that whenever you find a great church, it will be led by a pastor who is an effective preacher of the Word and also has learned to make wise choices of staff and lay leaders.

On the other hand, in countless churches growth has plateaued. Often this is due to poor choices in the placing of persons in leadership positions.

Think about your own ministry—how your staying in an assignment or moving to a new place affected you, your spouse, your family, and the people where you served. As you in turn have assigned persons to leadership roles, those decisions have also influenced many lives.

One of the greatest contributions Barnabas made to the Kingdom was to discover and nurture leaders. When Saul of Tarsus returned to Jerusalem after his conversion, the disciples "were all afraid of him, not believing that he really was a disciple. But Barnabas took him and brought him to the apostles" (Acts 9:26-27).

Barnabas believed in Saul. He persuaded the other disciples that Saul's conversion was genuine and that Saul had fearlessly preached about Jesus in Damascus. Barnabas then accepted Saul as his ministry partner. Saul was to become Paul—the greatest leader of the Early Church.

When John Mark "left the ministry" on the first missionary journey, it was Barnabas who gave Mark a second chance. We have Mark's Gospel today because Barnabas saw his potential.

When I was pastoring, my church had grown to the point that we were ready to employ a youth pastor. I became aware of a youth pastor who was not rehired by a church on another district where he was serving. He was devastated by being fired and decided to try changing careers.

He had heard of an opening for a probation officer in our community. When he came to interview, my wife and I met him and his wife for lunch. We discovered them to be persons of real character—a deeply committed Christian couple. They had a strong marriage and a genuine love for people—especially youth. It was evident to us that they would follow Christ regardless of their career choice.

I made phone calls to find out what had gone wrong in his previous church. I discovered from several sources that the senior pastor had not taken the time to work with him. This youth pastor was "on his own" with no feedback or support. I approached the young man with the idea of his interviewing with our church board. His first response was, "No, I failed as a youth pastor." After he and his wife prayed about it, he agreed to take this step just to see what would develop.

After they met with our teens and parents and our church board, it was clear that God was in it. His response to our call was "I'll give it a try—one more time!"

For eight years the Lord used him and his wife to build a dynamic youth group. They became our close friends and valued partners on our ministry team. He taught the young people (including our own children) to get into the Word. He continually encouraged high school graduates from our church and from the community to attend our regional denominational college. Even though the college was 225 miles away, there was one year when we had 41 students enrolled. What an impact his ministry had on our city!

When I became district superintendent, he felt led to accept a senior pastorate. He has become an outstanding preacher and a strong influence for Christ in his present community. When I think about his ministry and friendship, I feel a deep gratitude in my heart for God's amazing guidance.

One of the most important responsibilities of a Christian leader is calling pastors or staff members to positions of leadership. In church leadership development during the past two decades, several significant changes have occurred. Two major changes include

1. A marked increase in the number of paid pastoral staff;
2. A great growth in the number of volunteer lay leaders doing the work of ministry.

The increase in leaders becoming paid pastoral staff is very noticeable. For example, on one denominational district, research revealed the following:

- In 1975 there were 8 churches employing a total of 10 paid staff.
- In 2000 there were 20 churches employing 46 paid staff members.

The number of churches growing to become "large" churches accounted for some of the increase. But in 1975 there was only one church averaging fewer than 175 in attendance that had paid staff. By 2000, 9 churches averaging less than 175 had hired staff members. *Today, middle-size as well as large churches are employing staff.*

During these years we have also seen a phenomenal growth in the number of volunteer lay ministers. The churches are awakening to one of the basic tenets of the Protestant Reformation—*the priesthood of all believers.* The apostle Peter writing to Christians reminds them, "You also, as living stones, are being built up as a spiritual house for a holy priesthood, to offer up spiritual sacrifices acceptable to God through Jesus Christ" (1 Pet. 2:5, NASB).

Pastor Jim Garlow of Skyline Wesleyan Church in San Diego

says that when he was minister of lay development at a church in Oklahoma, he began making a list of all ministries in that church. They were averaging about 2,000 in attendance. Jim writes that he was shocked to find no fewer than 1,471 weekly ministries functioning in the church—all opportunities for laypersons to actively use their gifts for the Kingdom. Jim then discovered a resistance from some denominations to getting the laity involved. It centered on the misperception of who should do ministry.

On the surface there might seem to be a contradiction between needing more lay leaders and hiring more staff. The connection comes because the role of the staff is changing. A primary role of paid staff today is to recruit and equip the laity to do the work of ministry.

Years ago during searches for senior pastors or paid staff members, the focus was on those who could "do the job." Today in searching for senior pastors and staff, a key quality looked for is the leader's ability to mobilize laypersons to minister and reach the community.

This book is written to assist senior pastors and district/conference leaders in making wise and informed choices when recruiting paid pastoral leaders. The information provided in this book is primarily from two sources. First is the Bible, especially principles derived from the life of Jesus Christ and the writings of His key leaders—Paul, Peter, and John.

Second is my own experience as a paid staff member, as a senior pastor with multiple staff, and as a district superintendent. An ongoing valuable resource has been learning from other superintendents, senior pastors, and church board members.

In this book I will be suggesting principles for choosing leaders and a process of evaluating and interviewing. While the steps in the process are very specific, *my way is not the only way.* Your way of calling leaders may be an improvement over mine. What I am suggesting has worked well for me, and if you are able to adapt some of my ideas to your situation and they are helpful to you, I will have accomplished my purpose in writing.

To help avoid confusion I offer the following definitions:

- "Caller" will refer to the person who is primarily responsible for recommending candidates. This will typically be senior pastors or district/conference leaders.
- "Prospects" are those considered in the initial stages of the process.
- "Candidates" will refer to those who are definitely interested and whom the caller regards as having potential.
- "Serious candidates" are those whom the caller considers to be among the two or three candidates who have many of the right abilities and are open to an interview.
- "Reference" is a person contacted who has served with the candidate and is willing to share with the caller how he or she evaluates the candidate's character and abilities.
- "Chair" will refer to the person presiding over the church board (or search committee in some churches). If a staff position is being considered, the senior pastor will be the chair. If the vacancy is for a senior pastor, the chair will be the district/conference leader or a person appointed by this leader.

As you read the following pages, my hope is that you will find the principles and process helpful in your adventure of building a great team.

What to Look For in Candidates

In George Barna's perceptive book *Boiling Point—Monitoring Cultural Shifts in the 21st Century,* he offers the following observation:

> Your values determine who you are—your character, your relationships, your career choices, your lifestyle, your morals—this is a matter of huge importance. WHAT CAN YOU DO? Identify your core values. . . . Write down the values that are most important to you—the ones that you believe are critical to being who God wants you to be. . . . Get serious about your understanding of and commitment to God's truth principles.[1]

Whenever we need to fill a leadership position, it is an opportune time to reflect on what principles really matter to us. *Our core values will influence not only how we live but also what we regard as important in the leaders we choose.*

Dale Galloway suggests that the senior pastor should first clarify his or her own values and vision. In his book *Building Teams in Ministry,* he suggests a strategy that has worked for him. He urges every pastor to "First develop a vision, and then create a master plan to make the vision a reality. Then add only those staff people who fit your master plan."[2]

BIBLICAL CORE VALUES TO GUIDE THE CALLER

The following six biblically based core values are what I have regarded as important in prospective leaders. Framed as questions, these values focus on what to look for when choosing leaders and are incorporated into the guide sheets provided at the end of this book.

Core Value No. 1: Does the Candidate Have the Right Priorities?

The Bible teaches that we are to live according to an order of priorities. This is expressed in Christ's Great Commandment and Great Commission. I am suggesting that His order for us is as follows:

1. *God first:* "Love the Lord your God with all your heart" (Matt. 22:37).
2. *The family:* "Love your neighbor" (Matt. 22:39).
    a. At home: "Husbands, love your wives" (Eph. 5:25).
    b. The church family: "Christ loved the church" (Eph. 5:25).
3. *Our witness to the world:* "Go and make disciples of all nations" (Matt. 28:19).

Our commitment to God should be our highest priority. Jesus was asked, "Which is the greatest commandment?" He replied, "Love the Lord your God with all your heart and with all your soul and with all your mind. This is the first and greatest commandment" (Matt. 22:37-38).

The account of a candidate's conversion, how he or she came to repentance and faith, is significant. Regardless of the candidate's personality, there should be an evident assurance of the reality of his or her experience of salvation. But in addition, we should discern whether or not the candidate has a *wholehearted commitment to God.* This is consistent with the biblical teaching about living a Spirit-filled life—a life fully dedicated to God (see Acts 6:3; Rom. 12:1-2; and Eph. 5:18, NASB).

Bill Bright, the late founder of Campus Crusade for Christ, explained to Josh McDowell and a group of students how to be filled with the Holy Spirit by faith. Referring to 1 Cor. 2:14—3:3, he said, "There are three kinds of people in the world. The Bible tells us there is the natural man . . . who hasn't received the Lord Jesus as Savior. The carnal man . . . who has received Christ, but lives a defeated life. . . . But the spiritual man places Christ on the throne of his life, and his own ego steps aside to allow God's Holy Spirit to control his life." Josh McDowell responded afterward, "Never will I say I don't know how to be filled with the Spirit. . . . My life has never been the same since that night."[3]

A ministerial candidate needs to have made that surrender of self-centeredness in order to "love God with all [the] heart." If material things or relationships with people should surface as more important than the Lord, it's a clear warning to move on to another candidate. More often this is discovered only when questioning references. Asking the candidate to share his or her testimony with you will also usually help you begin to evaluate how committed the candidate is to God.

The family at home should be next in our order of priorities. Jesus said that the second commandment is to "love your neighbor" (Matt. 22:39). If we are married, it is obvious that our closest neighbor is our spouse. The apostle Paul stated in Eph. 5:25, "Husbands, love your wives, just as Christ loved the church." I enjoy misquoting this verse as "Husbands, love your *work* as Christ loved the church." We husbands tend to put our work ahead of our commitment to our spouses.

One of my professors in college, Paul Culbertson, once asked our class, "What is the greatest thing that a father can do for his children?" His answer was summed up in two words, "Love Mother!" He reminded us that children find their greatest security in Dad's and Mom's love and respect for each other. Any prospective pastor, staff person, or lay leader should have a strong marriage. A failure here will destroy the family and the church.

What about a parent's relationship to his or her children? Paul in 1 Tim. 3:4 emphasizes a prerequisite to serving as an overseer in the church: "He must manage his own family well and see that his children obey him with proper respect."

Once I was at a conference with pastors and staff listening to a speaker state, "After putting God first, there is no order to your priorities!" As I inwardly evaluated what he said, I acknowledged that the order *does* change. Sometimes there is a hospital visit or soul-winning encounter that must come before family. But I concluded that there still *is* an order. I thought to myself that if I could talk to the speaker's children, they could tell me where they ranked on their dad's priority list.

When I received my call to ministry, one of the earnest prayers of my wife and me was that our children would be saved. We knew it would be tragic to focus so much on winning other people that we would lose our own kids. As with all Christian parents, we faced some crucial challenges as our children grew up.

I thank God for James Dobson's far-reaching influence around the world to strengthen family life. In his recent best-selling book *Bringing Up Boys,* he recognizes the alarming absence of wise counsel from parents. So many children face times of crisis and come home battered from school. He states,

> Today's kids have nowhere to go with their rage. Some resort to drugs and alcohol, some withdraw into isolation, and some, sadly, vent their anger in murderous assault. If only mom or dad had been there when the passions peaked. So many of the difficulties that confront our kids come down to that single characteristic of today's families: There is nobody home.[4]

I realize that the minister and his or her spouse sometimes must work outside the home to pay the bills. Being bivocational or part-time is required in many cases. But what Dr. Dobson is saying is that either the minister or his or her spouse needs to make every effort to be there when the kids are home. "Being there" for our children provides them not only opportunities to build memories together but also a lifelong example of their importance to us. When they are grown, they will still want us involved in their lives.

When Judi, our daughter, was in sixth grade, she made friends with a girl who was a bad influence. Judi began to be despondent. My wife and I recognized that she was in a time of crisis and prayed fervently for her.

One day after Judi came home from school, my wife, Pollie, said to her, "Judi, let's go kick a rock around the block!" Judi said, "OK!" As they walked, they talked. At one point Judi stopped, looked at Pollie, and asked, "Mom, what's wrong with me? I'm so unhappy!" Divinely led, Pollie responded, "Judi, there's a battle going on inside you between Jesus and Satan. Both of them want you."

Then with loving conviction Pollie said, "Judi, Satan is *not* going to have you!"

At these words, Judi fell into Pollie's arms weeping. Judi poured out an earnest prayer. The peace that only Christ can give flooded her heart.

Judi's life was transformed. Her grades at school improved. Her cooperation in the home became evident. She has grown up to be a joy to us and a blessing for Jesus—a loving wife, a wise mother, and an effective registered nurse.

All of us who are parents should regard our relationship to our children as more important than our work. Even so, some parents who have kept the right priorities still have children who rebel against the Lord. Each child has the power of choice and can choose to go his or her own way. Despite this, we can continue to commit our children to God in prayer. Many do return to Him in later years—praise His name!

When we are considering a candidate, it is essential that we inquire about how healthy the prospect's relationship is to his or her spouse and children.

The church family should be the next priority to consider. Paul made it clear that "Christ loved the church and gave himself up for her" (Eph. 5:25). Paul also stated in Gal. 6:10, "Let us do good to all people, especially to those who belong to the family of believers."

Prospective leaders should have genuine love for their church. If leaders nurture Christ's kind of caring for each other within the congregation, then when newcomers come, they will be drawn to that church.

A leader in my denomination, Steve Weber, told me a most remarkable story of a lay leader's love for her church. Sarah Schubert, whose funeral Dr. Weber had recently attended, was the wife of Richard Schubert, president of Bethlehem Steel and for several years of the American Red Cross. Wherever Richard and Sarah were located, they became active in serving Christ in their local church.

When Richard was appointed by the president of the United States to be undersecretary of labor, the Schuberts moved to Washington, D.C. Upon finding that the young people of the church they attended did not have sponsors, they offered their services to the pastor. During this time the following incident occurred, as related by a friend at Sarah's funeral.

Shortly after the Schuberts arrived in Washington, the phone rang at their home, and Sarah answered. "This is the White House secretary to the president of the United States calling. The President has asked me to invite you and your husband to dinner at the White House this Friday evening." Sarah responded, "We're honored by this invitation, but we won't be able to come. We've committed ourselves to having the young people of our church at our house this Friday night. We wouldn't want to disappoint them!"

At the funeral, the friend stated, "Sarah turned down having dinner with the president of the United States because she valued her church's teenagers." His closing comment was "This lady had her priorities right!"

This kind of love for the church moves me deeply! When I'm tempted to allow my "church work" to become routine, I think of Sarah.

Our witness to the world is also to be a priority. In His Great

Commission, Jesus called leaders to "Go and make disciples of all nations" (Matt. 28:19). Effective leaders will do more than "shepherd the flock." They will go after the lost sheep (Luke 15:4-7). Jesus said that there is great joy in heaven when even one lost sheep is brought home.

I believe that one of the greatest joys we can experience here on earth is to lead an unbeliever to accept Christ as Savior. The expression of peace on the face of a newborn Christian is worth all the prayer, the caring, and the suffering love. *Nothing will impact a church, a youth group, or a Sunday School class like the testimony of a new person whose life has been transformed from darkness to light.*

Admittedly, not all Christian leaders have the gift of evangelism, but every leader is to be a witness, which should result in influencing some to be saved. A key question to ask references is "Has the candidate been instrumental in leading people to Christ?"

Core Value No. 2: Is There a Clear Call to Ministry?

It is true that every believer in the congregation is called to minister. But Eph. 4:11 identifies specific calls for "some to be prophets, some to be evangelists, and some to be pastors and teachers."

Why is a clear call to ministry so crucial? Perhaps an illustration about our son Dave will answer the question. A momentous phone call came to me from Dave when he was a junior in college. From his very first words I knew something extraordinary had happened. I asked my wife to pick up the other phone. Haltingly, with deep emotion, Dave said, "Dad, Mom . . . I just left the college prayer chapel. . . . I want to let you know . . . I believe God is calling me into the ministry!" We rejoiced with him and praised God for making His call so definite to our oldest son.

Years later, after his serving on staff and pastoring in several difficult situations, I asked Dave, "What held you steady during those times of trouble?" His answer: "Well, at first I pled with the Lord to allow me to become a mail carrier." Then he got serious and said, "The only thing that I knew for certain in those seasons of suffering was that *God had called me. God's call carried me through!"* Dave is now enjoying a fulfilling ministry as the family life associate pastor in a dynamic church.

Most of us would agree that God's call to ministry keeps us from giving up when the battle gets tough. A call to pastoral leadership is more than just choosing one of any number of careers. Granted, the call comes in different ways to different people. But there needs to be a sense that it is a divine call—that this is God's will for my life.

When considering leaders for a position, their assurance that God has called them is essential. Every candidate should be encouraged to respond to the invitation "Tell me about your call to the ministry."

Core Value No. 3: Whose Church Is It? Allow Christ to Build His Church.

Fresh out of seminary, my wife and I planted a new church in Phoenix. We held church services for a year in our parsonage and then started building on our church property. I began working five-and-a-half days per week constructing the building. I reserved one afternoon each week to prepare my Sunday sermons.

One Thursday afternoon I was getting nowhere with my sermons. I began to get irritated with God and prayed, *Lord, here I'm tired of body, building the church, and I need Your messages—fast!* I finally decided to put aside the books of sermons and to look into the Bible for something that "would preach." My eyes fell on the words in Matt. 16:18—five words from Jesus that transformed my ministry—"I will build my church."

Jesus let me know that it was *His* church—not mine. And He reminded me that if I would stop fretting, He could even use *me* to help Him build His Church. I was to stop burning the candle at both ends and take more time for prayer, my family, and sermon preparation. In that moment a big, heavy burden rolled off my shoulders. An encounter with the Head of the Church changed my ministry.

From time to time, leaders need to keep on giving themselves and their work back to God. A professor at a Christian university shared with me a story about the chaplain, Reuben Welch. One day he saw Reuben coming out of the campus prayer chapel, wiping tears from his eyes. Being a close friend, the professor went up to Reuben and asked, "Is there something that I can pray with you about?" Reuben replied, "Aw, no. For the umpteenth time I was giving this dumb university back to the Lord!"

This kind of transparent honesty has been refreshing and helpful to me on my life's journey. We, too, as leaders tend to revert back to carrying the load ourselves. We need an ongoing reminder to give our ministry back to Jesus.

Our son Dan has a deep love and respect for his pastors. At times he has seen his pastors get burdened down in their work. Two of his former pastors have burned out of the ministry. As a medical doctor, he often speaks to pastors and staff in retreats across the United States. In his recent book *Time Bomb in the Church—Defusing Pastoral Burnout*, he concludes with these heartfelt words:

> As a physician, I write prescriptions. May I write one for you and deliver it as a prayer?
>
> *Dear God . . .*
>
> *Renew Your ministers as they obey Your command to practice Sabbath rest, regularly. . . .*
>
> *Encourage them to address any lifestyle pattern that adversely affects their health, their marriage, their family, or their ability to minister Your way. . . .*
>
> *Refresh the ones You have called with a new awareness that You do not require unreasonable, imbalanced, or unhealthy service. . . .*
>
> *In the name of Jesus, our ministry Model and Enabler, Amen!*[5]

Core Value No. 4: Does the Candidate Make Prayer Primary?

When we are looking for a leader to fill an open position, it's a good time to deepen our own relationship with God. The prayer that we continually offer is for God's guidance, "O Lord, who do You have for this place?"

James S. Stewart in his classic book *The Life and Teaching of Jesus Christ* tells of the priority that Jesus placed on prayer. He wrote,

There was a day when the first apostolic band had to be chosen and the momentous decision made about the right men for carrying on His work. Luke, describing the night before the decision, says "Jesus went out into a mountain to pray, and continued all night in prayer" (6:12).[6]

My first district superintendent had two locations in mind when he called us to plant a church in Phoenix. When we traveled from Kansas City, we thought we would be going to Paradise Valley. When we arrived, the district superintendent said to us, "Last night on my knees, the Lord revealed to me that you should start in Deer Valley."

He was right! Deer Valley was ripe for the harvest. Many new converts were won to Christ. I will always be grateful for this district leader's example. He was a man of prayer, and he inspired me to rely upon God in my own prayer life.

Ronnie Floyd has written a great book titled *How to Pray*. He was among the speakers at the Promise Keepers 1997 "Stand in the Gap" event in Washington, D.C. It may have been the largest gathering of Christians in the history of the world. On the evening before this event, Dr. Floyd told how God's anointing came upon the leaders as they prayed for one another. Looking back on that significant gathering, Dr. Floyd wrote, "One of the reasons 'Stand in the Gap' was so powerful in the lives of many Christians was that the power of God first fell upon the leadership."[7]

When you question candidates about the place of prayer in their lives, do you sense that it is primary? Do they take time daily to rely upon God?

Core Value No. 5: Is There a Balance in the Candidate Between Authority and Accountability?

Jesus gives spiritual authority to His leaders. Among His last words to His disciples as recorded in the Gospel of Matthew were

"All authority in heaven and on earth has been given to me. Therefore go and make disciples of all nations" (28:18-19). Jesus has passed on His authority to us.

One of Paul's Gentile converts by the name of Titus became a capable and resourceful leader. Paul left Titus on the island of Crete for the purpose of organizing the churches. Paul later wrote an inspired letter to Titus. He instructed Titus to "appoint elders in every town" (Titus 1:5). Paul then described the qualities to look for in elders. He concluded his teaching with the admonition for leaders to "encourage and rebuke with all authority" (2:15).

When we consider calling a prospective leader, do the references agree that he or she preaches or teaches with spiritual authority? Some leaders have dynamic personalities. Others may be more soft-spoken. But whatever their personalities, *it is essential that they convey their convictions with a heartfelt spiritual authority that is grounded in God's Word.*

Having spiritual authority does not mean that the preacher or teacher is to be authoritarian. *Effective leaders are willing to be accountable.*

Jesus appointed 72 leaders beyond the 12 disciples. He gave them instructions and spiritual authority. But He also directed them to return and report back to Him, as inferred in Luke 10:17. They were held accountable.

Paul and Barnabas had great spiritual authority, but they knew they were also to be accountable. Acts 15:4 records how they returned from their first missionary journey: "When they came to Jerusalem, they were welcomed by the church and the elders, to whom they reported everything God had done through them."

Some pastors, staff, or lay leaders let their authority go to their heads. They see themselves as the "boss." Some get into financial or moral trouble because they are not willing to be accountable. Countless examples of persons no longer in the ministry could be cited. They failed to recognize that accountability can be a safeguard and a protection.

The senior pastor is to be accountable to the church board and district/conference leadership. Staff members are to be accountable to the senior pastor. And effective lay leaders are willing to answer to the staff or senior pastor.

In choosing leaders, it is wise to determine whether the candidate understands the need of a balance between authority and accountability.

Core Value No. 6: Does the Candidate Relate Well to People?

When I was a pastor and a district superintendent, one of my highest privileges was to develop friendships with pastors, staff, and lay leaders. Author Alan Loy McGinnis in his best-selling book *The Friendship Factor* documents the importance of relationships: "Studies at the Carnegie Institute of Technology reveal that even in such fields as engineering, about 15 percent of one's success is due to one's technical knowledge, and about 85 percent is due to skill in human engineering—to personality and the ability to lead people."[8]

Charles Osborne suggests why the tenure in ministry assignments is so brief: "Some ministers have as much difficulty with relationships as do members of their congregation. That is one of the reasons why the average pastorate in most denominations is around three years."[9]

Whenever I read Jesus' words in John 15:15, I am always amazed at how He regarded His disciples. Jesus said to them, "I no longer call you servants, because a servant does not know his master's business. Instead, I have called you friends, for everything that I learned from my Father I have made known to you."

One day while pastoring, I experienced just how much friendship really mattered. A youth pastor contacted me to inquire if I might hire him on my pastoral staff. I asked him how it was going where he was presently serving. He replied, "The youth group is growing. The parents are very supportive, and the church pays me well."

"Why in the world would you even consider moving?" I asked.

"Because," he said, "I'm not included in the pastor's circle of friends."

This is a definite reminder that the main reason a staff member chooses to accept a call to a church is that he or she senses a good relationship with the senior pastor. Staff members must have confidence in the character of the pastor and feel the pastor's friendship.

Eph. 4:12 gives us another reason for relating well to others: "to prepare God's people for works of service, so that the body of Christ may be built up." As leaders, *our friendships should result in discipling others to build Christ's Church.*

Pastor Dale Galloway, who helped build a significant church in Portland, Oregon, has written an excellent book, *Building Teams in Ministry.* He appeals for a revolution to mobilize the laity for leadership. He writes, "No church has enough resources to hire enough people to do all the work that is needed. Recruiting, motivating, equipping, and involving lay persons in ministry should be a part of every staff pastor's assignment."[10] Galloway's book offers some practical ways to multiply ministry through lay ministers. He has several outstanding coauthors, who provide plans to implement lay ministry.

When checking out a candidate to be a pastor or staff member, ask references about his or her ability to recruit and equip workers. A candidate's relational skills will largely determine how successful he or she will be in mobilizing lay ministers. In the "doing" of ministry, even the morale of the volunteers will be influenced positively by a leader whom they regard as their friend.

I have proposed that these six core values are of utmost importance when considering candidates for leadership. There may be others that are important to you. Identifying core values in the candidates whom we call will help us evaluate who they are—their character and their abilities.

As stated earlier, these values are incorporated into the guide sheet questions included in the appendix at the end of this book.

For review, the core values to look for in the choosing of leaders include the following:

1. Right priorities
2. A clear call to ministry
3. Allowing Christ to build His Church
4. Making prayer primary
5. A balance of authority and accountability
6. Relating well to others

The six biblical core values apply to calling staff members as well as calling pastors. However, you may want to add some attributes that are more uniquely required in particular staff assignments.

WHAT SENIOR PASTORS LOOK FOR IN PROSPECTIVE STAFF

I contacted five outstanding senior pastors[11] and requested that they respond to the question "What do you look for when you are considering the hiring of church staff?"

Pastor No. 1 has 14 paid staff members for his large, growing congregation. This pastor observes,

> There are three things I look for in the hiring of ministerial staff:
>
> 1. A heart for God
> 2. A teachable spirit
> 3. A servant's heart
>
> I have found that anyone with these qualities can grow into an assignment and accomplish much for the Kingdom. In researching the candidate, I would have already determined whether the person had many of the necessary gifts and skills for the assignment. It is so important to me that staff be a *part of a team*. I really don't want any "lone rangers" working with me.

Pastor No. 2 looks for four *C*s when considering staff. He states,

A CALL to ministry is fundamental. When he or she goes through troubled times and "hits the wall," only a divine call will hold him or her steady.

CHARACTER is the most important. . . . A potential staff member must have a track record of loyalty to leadership, a strong work ethic, integrity of life and speech, understanding of spiritual authority, and a teachable spirit.

Next I consider CHEMISTRY of my staff . . . does the potential staff member's gift mix, personality, and talents complement mine as pastor and those of the staff?

The final quality is COMPETENCY. The most important competency skill for a staff member is "leadership development." . . . The local church cannot afford to hire people to do ministry. It is the role of the [staff] pastors to equip the church for ministry. If they build strong people around them, their ministry will grow.

Pastor No. 3 summarizes what he considers to be important in selecting staff:

- I look for passion displayed in a heart for God.
- They need an energy level that drives them to accomplish great things for God.
- I want a "quality of spirit" revealed by a teachable heart. I honestly have been most successful when hiring from within our church.

Pastor No. 4 desires the following characteristics:

- When I'm searching for quality staff, the first thing that I'm looking for is a "whatever it takes" attitude. It's important to me that staff have an attitude that's both Christlike and positive.
- The second thing I'm looking for is technical skills and abilities with a special touch toward the people emphasis.

Pastor No. 5 looks for the following primary qualities when considering pastoral staff:

1. A vibrant personal faith in Christ, the ability to communicate aliveness to coworkers and congregation, a high energy level, gifts and experience that match job description and ministry goals, a sense of humor and a joy in living life.

2. A strong commitment to the senior pastor's vision/philosophy of ministry, compatible with pastor's leadership style, proactively loyal, willing to be held accountable.

3. A long-term commitment, knowing there is a period of adjustment and building relationships, and that lasting growth does not usually occur without an investment of 5-10 years.

4. A spouse (where applicable) who is supportive of ministry goals—staff and spouses are to positively participate in the total life of the church (attendance in the services, celebrations, board retreats, and so on).

SUMMARY

As we reflect on what district superintendents and senior pastors are looking for in pastors and staff, I'm reminded of a perceptive quotation by Jim Collins in his book *Good to Great.*

In determining "the right people," the good-to-great companies placed greater weight on character attributes than on specific educational background, practical skills, specialized knowledge, or work experience. Not that specific knowledge or skills are unimportant, but they viewed these traits as more teachable (or at least learnable).[12]

From the responses of the senior pastors, it is evident that there are basic character attributes that all effective Christian leaders have in common. Whether they're senior pastors or staff members, they should have *a genuine, lived-out commitment to Jesus Christ.* There must be that *divine call to be God's leader* in order to make a difference in the world. The second attribute, expressed in the Great Commandment, *is a sincere love for people*—our neighbors. Relating well to others and a real caring for their eternal destiny is a requirement for all Christian leaders.

34

While each senior pastor expressed his or her own unique description of what to look for, there are other recurring requirements, such as *being teachable, being a team player, having a high energy level,* and *possessing loyalty to authority.*

The priority that Jesus and the apostle Paul placed upon calling leaders is an example for us today. District/Conference leaders and senior pastors who are willing to learn how to become more effective in recruiting the right leaders will see Christ's kingdom grow—both in number and in spiritual vitality.

The Most Important Premise for Evaluating Candidates

One of the most valuable lessons I've ever learned about calling leaders came at a conference for district superintendents. Our denomination's church growth director invited a speaker named Charles Ridley. Dr. Ridley is one of the foremost authorities on personnel recruitment in our nation. He is formerly of Fuller Theological Seminary and is now on the faculty of Indiana University.

The best predictor of future behavior

is past behavior.

At the conference, Dr. Ridley gave each of us a printed sheet with the heading "Twenty Keys to Accurately Evaluate Leadership Candidates." He then instructed us, saying, "Take your pen and draw an 'X' across No. 2 through No. 20. Don't even read the other 19. Just remember No. 1!"

Talk about getting our attention! He then had us read aloud

with him No. 1: "The best predictor of future behavior is past behavior."

Dr. Ridley proceeded to throw us a curve by stating, "The most inaccurate way of evaluating candidates is by references and interviews." As district superintendents, we depended upon choosing pastors by contacting references and doing interviews. Now we were really frustrated.

One district superintendent asked, "If the most inaccurate way of evaluating candidates is by references and interviews, what's the most accurate way?"

Dr. Ridley replied, "References and interviews."

He went on to explain: "The questions you ask references and the candidates you interview should be focused on *past behavior.*"

He then illustrated his premise by asking a district superintendent to come forward for a role-playing interview. Playing the part of the pastoral candidate, Dr. Ridley requested the district superintendent to ask him interview questions.

The district superintendent asked, "What would be your vision for this church if you were called here?"

Dr. Ridley turned to us in class and stated, "This is not a relevant question! Remember: *the best predictor of future behavior is past behavior.*"

With this reminder, he asked the district superintendent to begin the interview again. The district superintendent now framed the question, "What was your vision for your last pastorate and in what ways did you see your vision accomplished there?" Dr. Ridley responded, "Now you have it! You've applied the premise to *past* behavior. Your question is relevant!"[1]

Across the years I've found this premise to be true. If it's kept in mind when asking questions of references and candidates, it can *accurately* predict the future behavior of candidates in all kinds of leadership positions.

For example, as a pastor whenever I had a new family arrive who had transferred from another church, I often made a phone call to their previous church and inquired about their involvement. If I received a positive report about their effectiveness from several who served with them in leadership, I would proceed without delay to offer them some leadership role. If I was informed that they did not do well or had relational problems, I would go very slowly in involving them.

When considering candidates for pastorates, staff positions, or lay leadership—does this mean that those *not* successful in a previous assignment should *never* be considered? No, there are some situations in which you discover that the candidate should not be held responsible for a perceived failure. But when a negative report is received, it's wise to check with several *additional* reputable references to determine the *real* story.

What if the *real* story does reveal some failure for which the candidate is responsible? Should he or she always be eliminated from consideration? No! I believe that sometimes people *do* change. But I've found that two observations are helpful here. First, what is the candidate's attitude toward a past problem? Does he or she own up to his or her part and accept some responsibility for the failure? What would he or she do differently? The candidate's attitude can guide you on whether or not to proceed. Second, when those of us who are calling candidates discover a weakness in a candidate's past, we can remind the candidate that a similar situation may eventually occur in a new assignment. Also, if the candidate does become a part of our team, we can encourage him or her to seek our counsel. This may prevent another failure. Communicate your interest in the candidate and in his or her future effectiveness in the Lord's work.

How can this premise—"The best predictor of future behavior is past behavior"—be applied to college or seminary graduates who may not have a ministry track record? I have made it a practice to first phone a professor who is known to be a good judge of character—one who takes time to know students. I then find out where the prospect attended church. I phone the church to inquire if the prospect had served there in some capacity. If so, I would ask for names and phone numbers of those who had served with the prospect who would be objective references about the prospect's performance.

If, for example, the prospect served as a Sunday School teacher of sixth-graders, I would ask questions. "Was the teacher well-liked? Did the class grow in number? Did the teacher influence any of the class members to accept Christ? Did the pupils grow spiritually?" If I received yes answers to these questions, I was definitely interested. If the prospect, with all the demands of school, was also effective in some kind of ministry, this was a good indication that the prospect would likely do good work in a pastor or staff assignment.

Later in this book this basic premise—"The best predictor of future behavior is past behavior"—will find its way into the wording of the guide sheet questions that will be asked of prospects and references.

Working Closely with Church Boards

A cross the years, I have learned as a pastor and district leader to regard church board members as *partners in ministry*. When there is a leadership position to fill, it is a good opportunity to deepen the relationship between church board members and their chair.

In my denomination the senior pastor is the chair of the church board. The district superintendent is the chair of the church board when a senior pastor vacancy occurs. When there is a staff vacancy or a new position is to be considered, the senior pastor nominates the candidate to the church board. Other denominations may or may not have similar structures; some use search committees. What's important is how the person in the chair position relates to the local church's governing board or search committee when leadership changes occur. For the sake of discussion, I will use my denomination's structure to model this.

Whenever there is a resignation of a senior pastor or a pastoral staff member, I have found it a wise practice to schedule a special church board meeting within the first week following the resignation. *When a leader announces his or her leaving, fears and problems can develop. It is a good "preventative medicine" to head this off by meeting with the board promptly.*

A brief outline of a suggested agenda for that board meeting is as follows:

- Inform the church board that you will be working closely with them.
- Decide how you will bring a good closure with the outgoing pastor or staff. Clarify plans for a farewell (if appropriate) and financial considerations.
- Discuss together interim arrangements—who will fill the pulpit, who will lead the youth group, and so on.
- Give a brief overview of the process of calling another leader.

The process of finding the right leader is most successful when it is a shared responsibility with lay leadership.

After the resigning leader has moved on, the district/conference leader or senior pastor may be ready to begin the process of calling a new leader.

As I have worked with church boards, I have come to the conviction that the process of finding the right leader is most successful when it is a shared responsibility with lay leadership.

I have found it helpful for the chair to establish some principles with the board on "how we can work together." The following principles are included in condensed form in Guide Sheet No. 1 of the appendix, "Church Board Agendas for Calling a Pastor or Paid Staff Member."

1. The Holy Spirit leads church board members as well as district/conference leaders and senior pastors in the calling of leaders.

I remember well how the Spirit led one particular board member. We were in the process of calling a new senior pastor in a church on my district. One of the board members made it clear that he favored a candidate whom he had heard was a good pastor. When I made phone calls inquiring about the candidate, one reference expressed to me that this candidate was lacking in an area of ministry. When I reported the reference evaluation on this candidate and two other candidates, the board voted to interview one of the others. The candidate interviewed declined the board's nomination. The board interviewed the second of the other two candidates but did not nominate him.

Before the next board meeting I decided to check several other references on the third candidate—the one desired by the board member. I discovered that the one negative comment previously mentioned by a reference was *not* accurate. When I reported to the board these revised reports, they called the candidate for an interview.

At the interview with the candidate and his wife, it was clear that he was God's man for this church. After the board nomination and positive congregational vote, the candidate accepted the call. During his 13 years there as senior pastor, the church experienced spiritual and numerical growth. A spacious new sanctuary was built. He did a great work for the Lord. It was that board member's kind persistence that prompted me to get an accurate evaluation. I will always be grateful for him and for the many Spirit-led board members like him.

2. Clarify the roles of those responsible for calling leaders. Denominations differ in how this is done. It's important to consult your own church's manual or bylaws for the proper procedures and protocols.

3. Every board member's point of view is important.

Occasionally there will be one or two board members who dominate the discussion of a new senior pastor or staff candidate. When this occurs, it may be helpful for the chair to say, "How do some of the rest of you feel about this?" Sometimes when considering a major issue and input is needed from all the board members, a good approach is "I'd like each one to express his or her point of view. Let's start on this side and go around the table."

4. Express your point of view *in* the board meetings. Explain that division can develop if board members form into groups *outside* the meetings. Recommend that each board member withhold his or her judgment as to who should be interviewed until all the information is gathered.

These are four principles that, if agreed upon, can build trust among the board members and with the one who chairs the meetings.

Sometimes there is a tendency on the part of church board members to get in a hurry when the calling process begins. A board member may ask the chair in the first meeting, "Who do you know that would be a good candidate?"

This is an opportune time to respond, "Before we talk about who we will call, we need to consider two questions: 'Where are we as a church?' and 'What kind of leader do we need?'"

When there is a pastoral or staff vacancy, it is a good time to review and evaluate the local church. Guide Sheet No. 1, part B, refers to one of the scriptures that recognize the church as a "body." Explain that just as the physical body is alive and continually changing, so the church body is living and constantly changing.

If the chair becomes aware of a problem in the church, he or she should deal with it now *before* a new pastor or staff member comes.

Take time to discuss with the church board the issues raised in Guide Sheet No. 1, part B, dealing with "where are we as a church?" Remind them that when you start contacting pastoral or staff prospects on their behalf, the prospects will often say, "Tell me about the church!" Let the board know that your response to that request can be informed by the board members' perceptions.

It is helpful to apply the "Where are we?" question to that specific area of ministry for which the church is considering hiring staff. The staff member candidate will want to know about the strengths and concerns of his or her field of ministry.

I would make an important suggestion here: If the chair becomes aware of a problem in the church, he or she should deal with it now *before* a new pastor or staff member comes.

If the church has a record of being critical of pastors or staff, delay the process of calling a new pastor or staff member until the congregation has been confronted with their attitudes. Problems can often be more readily addressed when no personality is present. Arrange for a wise interim pastor or volunteer staff member to fill in for the time being. It is a tragedy when incoming pastors or staff become "sacrificial lambs" because they inherited a problem that should have been dealt with by leaders before they arrived. Some of those "sacrificed" end up leaving the ministry.

There may be time in the same board meeting to move on to Guide Sheet No. 2, "Church Board Agenda: What Kind of Leader Do We Need?" If you proceed, read the first section of chapter 4 beforehand. Or it may be wise to consider "What Kind of Leader Do We Need?" in the next board meeting.

It is helpful to have a job description. However, keep in mind that when the basic expectations are evident in a candidate, it is best to be flexible in *adapting* the job description to the unique gifts of a good candidate of character.

A job description will be helpful—especially in the calling of staff. You need not "start from scratch" in creating a job description. Stan Toler has compiled the *Church Operations Manual—A Step-by-Step Guide to Effective Church Management*. One section within it has job descriptions that can be copied and adapted to staff needs. There are job descriptions for executive pastor, associate pastor, youth pastor, children's pastor, minister of music, and church secretary.[1]

It is helpful to have a job description. However, keep in mind that when the basic expectations are evident in a candidate, it is best to be flexible in *adapting* the job description to the unique gifts of a good candidate of character.

Financial support for the candidate will need to be considered and approved by the church board. The level of support should include both "faith" and "reality."

Often finance committees will recommend to the church board a *total financial package*. This does give the candidate some flexibility in designating where his or her support should be directed. However, I have found that the committee and the board need to come to grips with specific expenses. They should take the time to arrive at *what will be a realistic figure* for housing and utilities, for health insurance, Social Security, auto reimbursement, tax-sheltered annuity, and salary. The "total package" approach is often just a shortcut to *save time* in a finance committee.

Sometimes a board member will say, "Wow—$35,000 total package. I wish I made that much!" In response to that statement, *remind the church board members that their total compensation is different from the pastor/staff total compensation.* For example, ask the board, "In your job are you asked to use your personal car for business purposes?" The minister *often* uses his or her auto 75 percent of the time for the church. Sometimes this expense is included in the minister's total package. Also, ask them, "Do you count your health insurance costs as a part of your total compensation?" Most of them do not.

Adequate compensation recommended and approved by the church board will allow the pastor or staff member to provide for his or her needs. It will enable him or her to focus attention on serving the church.

Note: The guide sheets included in the appendix at the end of this book will become relevant reading when you are actually facing a pastoral or staff vacancy. You will find them helpful forms to use when gathering information about prospects and candidates and when recording evaluations of references. There are also suggested outlines for church board agendas.

Locating and
Contacting Prospects

You may have received names of prospects at the end of the last church board meeting (refer to Guide Sheet No. 2). Or you may be accepting names during this next meeting. Regardless, before receiving names, convey to the board some important information, as follows.

Let the board members know that names of prospects for pastor or staff can come from three sources: (1) any in the congregation who recommend names to a board member or to the chair, (2) the board members themselves, or (3) the chair. If you are a senior pastor recommending the hiring of staff, your board may not have any names to suggest. They may rely solely upon yours.

You, as chair, may wish to offer your names in this board meeting. Or you may desire to receive any names that they suggest and then add your names later. Let the board know that in the process of making contacts, you may also be adding *other* names to the list.

Before opening up for the board members to offer their names of prospects, suggest that the only information needed in this board meeting is the names of prospects and their present location. Ask them *not* to offer their evaluation of the prospects at this point. They would have opportunity to do this at a later meeting.

Let the board know that the only reason you would *not* make contact with a prospect is if you discover that prospect has been in his or her present assignment for a very brief time. Remind them that we would not be building Christ's kingdom when we pull away a leader prematurely. District superintendents on our region even had a "gentleman's agreement" not to contact any prospective pastor who had been in his or her present assignment for fewer than three years—unless we contacted the pastor's district superintendent first to receive his approval. This policy brought a real sense of unity to our region. We worked as a team.

BUILD A PROSPECT LIST

In the days after receiving the prospects' names at the board meeting, the chair should wisely *expand* the prospect list.

To do this it is helpful to build a "support team" of discerning references who enjoy recommending effective pastors or staff persons. Within the same region, district leaders, pastors, laypersons, and wise and astute educators could all be included on such a team.

Whenever I had a pastor or staff vacancy, my first thought was *not* "Who would be a good candidate?" but "Who would be good references who know people?"

Contact those on your support team to describe the pastoral or staff vacancy, and then ask, "Do you think of anyone who might fit in this situation?"

Dale Galloway was very successful at hiring staff members from within his church. In *Building Teams in Ministry* he shares his insights in a chapter titled "Home Growing Your Staff." Galloway describes the advantages of senior pastors hiring paid staff from *within* the local church and from *without*. Some of his reasons are summarized as follows:

Advantages of Home Growing a Staff

- The advantage of observing their ministry gifts and relationships before you ask them to join the staff.
- Church members are willing to accept ministry from persons they already know.
- They may be willing to work part-time and not need much money because of pension, Social Security, and investment income.
- Insiders already have influence that allows them to get a quick start toward an effective ministry.

When to Hire from Outside

- When a church becomes ingrown and leaders may start to think alike.
- When you need a higher level of competence in an area where none exists.
- When creativity and new ideas run low.

Go outside when you need stronger leaders to take your church to higher levels of outreach and growth.[1]

District/Conference leaders when building a list of prospective pastors may find it helpful to divide it into two lists: "Prospects from Within My District" and "Prospects from Outside My District."

The "Prospects from Within My District" list would include staff members who may someday do a good work as a senior pastor. You may want to say to staff (as well as your most effective pastors whom you want to keep), "If you come to the place where you are open to a move, please let me know!" There are some advantages in calling pastors or staff from within your district. You may have first-hand knowledge of their strengths and weaknesses. You also may know whom you can depend on for accurate evaluations.

When district/conference leaders or senior pastors are looking for pastoral or staff prospects beyond their own districts/conferences, "support teams" should be comprised of persons who have a "Kingdom-wide" viewpoint and are concerned not just about building *their* church or district/conference.

Preliminary Research on Prospects

Once names of prospects are gathered, the district/conference leader or senior pastor should find out basic information about the candidates.

This information should be available through your denomination's district/conference or national/international headquarters. A district/conference journal may also be in use as a source of this information. In the Church of the Nazarene each district has its own district journal containing such details about ministerial prospects as the spouse's name, how long the person has served in the present assignment, home phone, and statistics of the church or youth/children's group, and the attendance in the year the person came and also at the most recent yearly district assembly. Guide Sheet No. 3 at the end of this book can be used to record information like this.

If the prospect's tenure is discovered to be too brief in his or her present assignment, the prospect may be eliminated from consideration. From denominational records you should be able to find a pastor's or staff member's starting dates. If not, a phone call may be necessary to find out how long he or she may have served. It's important to keep in mind that exceptional circumstances do exist that should *not* eliminate pastors or staff who are "short-timers."

Contacting Prospects

Reviewing a prospect's record on Guide Sheet No. 3 may reveal how interested you would be in him or her. For example, one indicator might be a significant increase or reduction in attendance. If everything has plateaued attendance-wise, check on how many persons joined by profession of faith. "None" would be a red flag.

"Many" might indicate that the leader is reaching new people, which will later result in overall growth.

Guide Sheet No. 4 is a suggested approach for your "Initial Phone Conversation with Prospect." After you have introduced yourself, let the prospect know the reason for your call. Ask, "Would you be open to hearing about this available position?" If the answer is no, thank the person graciously. He or she may be a possible prospect in the future.

If the prospect is willing to listen to your description of the position, he or she may decline further consideration by the end of your talk. But if the prospect is open to further discussion, consult Guide Sheet No. 4 for additional pertinent questions and dialogue. After reviewing the prospect's record and reflecting on your phone conversation, you may decide that he or she would be a candidate who warrants more serious consideration.

5

Evaluating Candidates Through References

The Early Church experienced phenomenal growth. It spread like wildfire across the civilized world. One of God's primary instruments in igniting the Spirit's purifying fire in the lives of people was the apostle Paul.

As you read the Bible account of Paul's missionary journeys, you become aware that this explosive growth was not dependent on Paul alone. *He had effective leaders to build Christ's churches.* Think about the names of some of them: Silas, Titus, Lydia the businesswoman, and Luke the physician, who was to write the Gospel of Luke and the Book of Acts. In the last chapter of Romans, Paul sends greetings to no fewer than 26 leaders. His first greeting is to a wife and husband, Priscilla and Aquila, to whom Paul refers as "my fellow workers in Christ Jesus" (Rom. 16:3).

How did Paul choose such effective leaders? Do the scriptures that tell of his calling of leaders give us any guidance today?

Look at Paul's call to one who was to become an outstanding staff member and later a pastor—Timothy. During Paul's second missionary journey Paul needed the right person to help him strengthen the churches. Acts 16 tells how he enlisted Timothy: "He came to Derbe and then to Lystra, where a disciple named Timothy lived, whose mother was a Jewess and a believer, but whose father was a Greek. The brothers at Lystra and Iconium spoke well of him. Paul wanted to take him along on the journey" (Acts 16:1-3).

THE EARLY CHURCH PATTERN
FOR EVALUATING CANDIDATES

Paul's call to Timothy in Acts 16:1-3 provides a pattern for us:

- *Gather background information.* Paul found a spiritual heritage on his mother's side—"whose mother was a Jewess and a believer."
- *Check with references where the candidate has served.* "The brothers at Lystra and Iconium spoke well of him."
- *Experience a personal bonding.* "Paul wanted to take him along on the journey."

As mentioned in the last chapter, background information may be secured by contacting your denominational headquarters—at the district/conference or national/international level. They have the records that will provide this basic information.

The personal bonding in the calling process can take place in the interview. This important contact between the candidate, the chair, and the church board will be discussed in the next chapter.

The most accurate evaluations of a candidate

will come from objective references.

However, neither the denominational records nor the interview will provide a very accurate assessment of a candidate's strengths and weaknesses. Interviews, for example, do not reveal how a minister deals with conflict or how successful he or she may be in evangelism and discipleship.

How did Paul get an accurate picture of Timothy? He sought out references from two churches where Timothy had served. This leads to the suggestion that the most accurate evaluations of a candidate will come from objective references.

To help church board members understand the value of objective references, I will say to them, "Suppose one of your pastors or staff members with whom you work closely were to take another ministry assignment in another church. Several years later, a district superintendent or a senior pastor phones you and says, 'I'm considering calling this minister to a church. I understand that you served with him [her]. I will keep your name confidential. Would you answer some questions about his [her] ministry?' If you agree to respond, and since you know the minister well, you could give an accurate evaluation . . . right? Now, suppose two other board members were also contacted. None of you know that others were phoned. All three of you give very *similar* responses to his questions. Would you agree that the district superintendent or senior pastor could conclude that 'this is a true picture of the candidate'?"

When this example is given, most board members will understand that objective references will usually be the most accurate and dependable source for evaluating candidates.

WHO IS AN OBJECTIVE REFERENCE?

Sometimes the accuracy of a reference's evaluation is questioned—and for good reason. We will not necessarily get an accurate evaluation just from contacting a *number* of references, but from *objective* references. We might phone three or four persons who had a slight acquaintance with the candidate and receive very inaccurate reports. One reference may have a negative attitude. Another might see all people through rose-colored glasses and think that leaders can do no wrong.

A key question, then, is *"Who is considered to be an objective reference?"* An objective reference is a person who

- served with the candidate in a previous church
- is well aware of his or her ministry
- is regarded as a good judge of character

Notice the statement "in a previous church." A reference from the *present* church should *not* be regarded as objective. If laypersons are asked to evaluate their present pastor or staff member, it will be difficult to get a true picture. If they like their leader, they will not want to lose him or her and might tend to give a more negative report. If they are not happy with their leader, they may offer a more positive report, hoping that he or she might leave. People are *human*. It is not fair to ask them to evaluate their present leaders.

Then again, the reference may have served with the candidate in his or her present church but has since moved away. This person may be a reference who could be very objective and offer a fair evaluation.

How to Find References Who Are Objective

We should readily admit that objective references are not easy to locate. It's hard work! And yet they are absolutely necessary if we're to get a true picture of a candidate.

I have observed that those responsible for calling leaders may tend to rely on a personal contact or a recommendation from only one reference. Yet to secure accurate evaluations from several objective references should be our highest priority.

How can we find references who are objective? One of the first references to consider may actually come from the candidate. Note that at the end of Guide Sheet No. 4, the interested prospect may be asked, "Are there any laypersons who served with you in a previous church who would be objective in their evaluation of your ministry? Or are there any who served with you in your present assignment who have moved away?" If the prospect responds "Yes," ask how long they worked with him or her and what their leadership positions were in the church. Request their present location and phone number.

It is obvious that candidates will usually suggest references who will give them *favorable* reports. These persons may or may not be objective. But they may be able to recommend other references. Ask them if they know of another person (who is not presently attending the church where the pastor or staff candidate is serving) who would be an objective reference. They may be able to give you a phone number or some other contact information.

Another possible resource is to contact the board secretary or treasurer of the previous church where the candidate served. Ask if he or she was attending there when the candidate served in that church. If so, ask the questions on Guide Sheet No. 5. Then inquire if he or she knows of others who worked closely with the candidate and who would give an objective evaluation. Request their phone numbers.

One other source for finding objective references can come from the "support team" list you may have compiled (see chapter 4). These are discerning district/conference leaders, pastors, or laypersons who are aware of the character and abilities of other pastors or staff. They may have been on the same district/conference where the candidate had served. Phone them to find out if they are familiar enough with the candidate to be an objective reference. They may also know some other references to contact.

What about a reference who gives a negative report on a candidate? I have made it a practice to identify the specific area of complaint and then make *additional* phone calls to find out the truth. For example, one reference told me, "He has a hang-up against any evangelistic invitations!" I phoned another trusted reference, and he concurred: "That's right—he won't allow any invitations for people to make a public commitment!" These two references influenced me to drop the candidate from being considered by a church that had a healthy attitude toward evangelism.

At other times, the negative report will *not* be accurate. By checking additional references who refute the first report, we clear a reputation and have a candidate who may make an outstanding pastor or staff member.

I want to make an important observation at this point. Often when I met at gatherings with other district superintendents and pastors, the subject of choosing leaders would come up. I could count on hearing the same old saying: "Get the right man in the right place at the right time!" Everybody always agreed.

But I soon discovered that not all superintendents or senior pastors actually took the time required to contact three or more objective references. Under the pressure of their work, they would settle for one report of someone who knew the candidate. Another quote from Jim Collins's *Good to Great* book reinforced my observation of how easy it is to fail to follow through.

> The main point is not just about assembling the right team—that's nothing new. . . . [The] point is the degree of *sheer vigor* needed in people decisions. . . . "First who" is a very simple idea to grasp, and a very difficult idea to do—and most don't do it well. It's easy to talk about paying attention to people decisions—but how many executives have the discipline to do it?[1]

If it requires discipline to select the right leaders in order to make a company profitable financially, how much more should we devote ourselves to checking out candidates who will have a spiritual and eternal impact on human lives?

This locating of objective references will take much time and effort. Is it worth it? Yes! The more accurate the evaluations that are collected, the greater the probability that the candidate called will be a "match."

The apostle Paul, with all the discerning gifts granted him by the Holy Spirit, still made inquiry about his prospective staff member Timothy. He contacted leaders in the two churches of Lystra and Iconium who had worked with young Timothy.

Guide Sheet No. 5 will provide the caller with suggestions on how to approach potential references. It also lists specific questions that should prove helpful in discerning abilities and attitudes. The questions are worded with this key premise in mind: "The best predictor of future behavior is past behavior."

When three or more evaluations by objective references on each candidate have been received, the senior pastor or district/conference leader is ready for the next step in the process.

Preparing for the Church Board Meeting

There are some important steps the district/conference leader or senior pastor should take prior to the church board meeting in which a candidate will be chosen for an interview.

First, *schedule a meeting when all (or nearly all) board members will be present.* The decisions made at this meeting may result in choosing a candidate for an interview. The presence or absence of one or two key board members will change the dynamics of the meeting. I know of a situation in which a church lost a good youth pastor candidate because two key board members could not be present. In the meeting some of the board members "got off on a tangent." The absent key leaders could have prevented this had they been present. If several board members will be unable to attend on a proposed date—reschedule the meeting.

Second, *prepare a folder for each board member.* Some chairs may consider this extra work unnecessary. But it will be something that the board members will appreciate because they can record important information about each candidate. Have a page that reminds the board of the top three qualities or roles in a candidate that the board regarded as primary (refer to Guide Sheet No. 2). A page for each candidate may be prepared with background information that was collected on Guide Sheet No. 3. Leave space on the lower half of the sheet for board members to take notes when you share information and the evaluations of references.

Third, in preparing for the board meeting, *organize your reference evaluations on each candidate.* Become familiar with the background information on Guide Sheet No. 3. Also, on Guide Sheet No. 4 assimilate the comments that you have recorded from the candidate. On Guide Sheet No. 5 give special attention to evaluation comments that you have recorded from objective references. From these guide sheet responses, you will often be able to project in advance which candidates the board will regard as serious candidates. Because of the trust level you have developed with the church board, they may ask you which candidate or candidates *you* would favor inviting for an interview.

A final step in preparing for the board meeting will be to *phone those whom you consider "serious candidates"* and ask, "If the church board should vote to invite you and your spouse for an interview, would you be willing to come? What two possible dates might fit into your schedule?"

The first section of Guide Sheet No. 6 will outline these four vital steps of preparation for the next board meeting.

REPORTING EVALUATIONS—A CRUCIAL BOARD MEETING

Section II of Guide Sheet No. 6 is a suggested agenda for the next church board meeting.

It has been my experience that when a candidate interviews with a church board, in the majority of cases the candidate will be called to the church. So this is a significant board meeting. It should be approached with careful preparation and prayer.

In the adventure of calling leaders, we can again rely on Jesus' promise "I will build my church" (Matt. 16:18). I believe Christ is pleased when we admit our dependence upon His guidance. So many lives will be influenced by the leader who is called to serve as a pastor or a staff member. This board meeting will be a special opportunity for the chair and the board members to experience together the Holy Spirit's leading.

Acts 16:1-3 is the biblical pattern for choosing leaders. This devotional outline on the agenda may be enlarged upon by referring to "Early Church Pattern for Evaluating Candidates" near the beginning of chapter 5. Emphasize the importance of evaluations by objective references. Give the example related in chapter 5 that if a district/conference leader or pastor were to request from them an evaluation of a leader with whom they had previously served—they could provide a true picture of that leader. This is the reason they should depend upon objective references as primary in evaluating candidates. Encourage the board members themselves to offer prayers asking the Lord for His guidance. Remind them of how Jesus prayed before choosing His leaders (Luke 6:12).

After the opening prayers, establish guidelines on how you will proceed together.

The first is that *candidates should be considered one at a time for an interview.* Explain to the board members that although they might fill a vacant position at their business by interviewing two or three top candidates and then choosing the best one, calling a pastor or staff member is different. Ministers usually are *not* seeking a job change. When they're contacted, allowing their name to be considered may simply be a *step* in finding God's will. Candidates may also ask, "Am I just one in a number of candidates that you will interview?" Candidates do not usually consent to an interview unless they sense that the chair and the church board are genuinely interested in them personally.

Another reason to avoid deciding on a candidate among multiple interviews is that it may tend to divide the board and the church. For example, one church board asked their two top candidates to come for interviews. When both had interviewed, some board members favored one candidate, and others favored the second one. When a vote was taken, it was split down the middle. Neither candidate would consider proceeding further. Two top candidates were lost—partly because of the process of competing interviews.

Admittedly, sometimes it is necessary to have competing interviews. But usually a better plan is to decide on which top candidate to call for an interview. Neither the church nor the candidate is *obligated* to accept the other. Assure the board that they will *not* be pressured to vote in favor or against—they will vote by ballot. If the board does not vote to nominate the candidate, they can consider another one. Sometimes the board interviews and nominates a candidate, but he or she does not feel clear in accepting. Then another candidate will be considered for an interview. The chair should remind the board that *both* the board and the candidate must receive a confirmation from the Lord.

Another understanding to have with the church board is that *the spouse should be invited to come to interview with the candidate.* It is important for the church to get to meet the spouse. The spouse's values and supportiveness of her husband or his wife should be explored. The spouse also needs to "experience the church." Often a move to this new location will involve children as well. Helpful information about where they will live and what schools they will attend are primary family issues. The best decisions are made when the candidate and the spouse agree together about their coming.

After covering these guidelines with the board, proceed by passing out "research folders" to each board member. Request that they write their names on the folders. Mention that they will be collected at the end of the board meeting—since they may write down comments on candidates that should be kept confidential within the board meetings. Let them know that their folders will be passed out to them again when they meet for an interview.

A second page may be included in their folders that summarizes the "kind of leader" they profiled on Guide Sheet No. 2. This identifies the roles or qualities desired in a leader. Suggest that when they consider the individual candidates, they keep these priorities in mind. For example, if "preacher/teacher" was a high priority, they should be looking and listening for that ability when reference evaluations are read. Request board members to make notes that will remind them of the candidate's strengths or weaknesses.

Recommend to the board that you read through the names in the folder three times. The first time, go over basic background information that you gathered on Guide Sheet No. 3. The second time, share responses of the candidates themselves from your phone conversations with them on Guide Sheet No. 4. The third time through the folder will be comments expressed to you by three or more objective references from Guide Sheet No. 5.

One more observation can be made about the value of using objective references to evaluate candidates. Sometimes among the prospect names are relatives of board members or of church members. Or a prospect may be a board member's close friend. The chair may be in deep trouble if he or she makes personal comments about the prospect that are *not* positive. But if the chair reads comments without identifying the references' names—the chair can be candid. Objective references provide a safeguard for the chair.

Evaluations from objective references provide a protection for the chair. Should the comments on a candidate be negative, the chair will not be blamed as their source.

After you have completed the reading of the "objective reference" evaluations, let the board know that you are open to questions or comments about any of the candidates. Often, several of the board members will zero in on one or two names. After you have discussed the candidates, the next direction the board wishes to take may be clear to you.

If you are a senior pastor seeking to fill a staff position, you may have only one candidate to consider. If the candidate has good references and you feel positive about him or her, the board will likely accept your recommendation that this person be interviewed. Should there be two or more candidates, one may clearly stand above the rest. You as chair may be asked which person you favor as the one to interview. Since the board has confidence in you, feel free to offer your recommendation, and ask if there is a motion to proceed on to an interview.

Often out of a list that may include five or more candidates, two or three may be ones whom you and the board regard as serious candidates. You may want to pass out ballots. Request that each board member write the name or names of those who have the qualities that are needed in a pastor or staff member. Have them pass in the ballots, and let the board secretary and an assistant tabulate them. Announce the results.

Now focus further on comments made by references concerning these two or three serious candidates. Then ask board members to write one name on a ballot. Let them know that the majority vote will be "our" vote for an interview. If it is not unanimous, remind them that *they can have unity without uniformity.* Ask them to approach the interview with an open attitude.

Guide Sheet No. 6, section II. D., will provide information on planning an interview date that will be best for both the church and the candidate.

Section II. E., offers one suggested schedule for the interview events. Plan whatever groups and times fit best for you. *The important thing is to plan gatherings that will give the candidate and his or her spouse ample opportunity to get well acquainted with the board and the church people.*

In reviewing what we have covered, the primary emphasis of this chapter is on gathering accurate evaluations from objective references. When the chair does his or her homework here, these evaluations will provide a true history of a candidate's ministry. The next steps in the interviewing process can then be approached with confidence.

Interviewing a Candidate

So far we have emphasized that objective references provide the caller with the most accurate evaluations of candidates. From objective references we learn of a candidate's commitment to Christ and his or her abilities, attitudes, and people skills.

However, reading résumés or making phone calls is not the same as meeting candidates face to face. When the apostle Paul called Timothy, he did not rely solely on the references from Iconium and Lystra. He met Timothy personally. He experienced a bond of friendship after this personal contact. Acts 16:3 says, "Paul wanted to take him along."

The opportunity for personal contact is what the interview is all about. God has created pastors, spouses, and churches with unique personalities. We all relate differently to one another. We "fit" better with some people than others.

I remember a pastoral candidate who came to interview with a church board. His record showed considerable growth where he had been serving for six or seven years. The references all gave very positive reports, and the board was unanimous on calling him for an interview. When my wife and I met him at the airport, after a few minutes of getting personally acquainted—our spirits sank. We sensed that he would not "fit" in this church. Perhaps it was his demeanor, which was at home in a rural setting but not this urban one.

I did not communicate my disappointment to the church board. He was a good man—a committed pastor. I simply prayed as he interacted with the board. When he excused himself at the end of the interview and I was alone with the board, one of the members spoke up. He observed, "This man has many fine qualities, but I don't think he would be a good match for our church." Other members of the board expressed that they felt the same way. I told them I agreed. I was relieved when they chose not to nominate him as pastor. It would not have been right for him or the church.

Sometimes the chair will need to take a risk and state his or her disapproval—even though the board has not discerned that the candidate will not fit. When the chair has built a trust level with the board, most board members will accept this.

It should be kept in mind that *the interview is as important to the candidate and his or her spouse as it is to the church.*

The interview serves a very significant function. It is an opportunity to discover whether or not there is a personal bonding of the candidate and his or her spouse with the church leaders and the congregation.

Consider using the following interview schedule. It will provide ample opportunities for getting acquainted.

- The chair meets with the candidate and his or her spouse to get to know them. As stated earlier, it is helpful if the chair's spouse can also be present. This could be a previous meeting or on the afternoon of the interview.
- Church board and spouses or pastoral staff and spouses meet

with the candidate and his or her spouse for a meal or light refreshments. This is a friendship time in which leaders introduce themselves to the candidate and his or her spouse.

- The chair interviews the candidate and his or her spouse before the entire congregation or a ministry group if this is a staff candidate. The chair asks about their family, their conversion, the candidate's call to ministry, and so on.
- A reception is given during which members of the congregation or ministry group have an opportunity to personally introduce themselves to the candidate and his or her spouse.
- The chair, candidate, and spouse meet with the church board for the official interview. Interaction and discussion are encouraged.
- After dismissing the candidate and his or her spouse, the chair meets with the church board to discuss their evaluation of the interview and to take appropriate action.

The candidate and his or her spouse will appreciate hearing from the chair about the above schedule *prior* to their coming for the interview. This will give them an overview of what to expect.

Guide Sheet No. 7 in the appendix will also outline the above schedule and give information on how to approach each meeting. For example, it includes some suggested questions for the chair to ask the candidate and his or her spouse at the interview. The chair may find it helpful to use Guide Sheet No. 7 as an outline throughout the interview process.

The remainder of this chapter will enlarge upon the reason for each meeting on the schedule and also provide some dos and don'ts.

CHAIR MEETS WITH CANDIDATE AND HIS OR HER SPOUSE

The importance of the meeting of the chair with the candidate and his or her spouse cannot be overemphasized. If the candidate is coming to interview for a staff position, the candidate's relationship to the senior pastor—the chair of the board—is primary. He or she will be on the senior pastor's "pastoral team." If the candidate is interviewing for a senior pastor vacancy, the district/conference leader—the chair in this case—will also want a candidate who will be a vital member of his or her "district/conference team."

The chair's spouse should be included in this initial meeting whenever possible. This will give him or her the opportunity to get to know the candidate and his or her spouse. The chair may also receive valuable insight from his or her spouse as to the candidate's and spouse's personalities and attitudes. Furthermore, the candidate and his or her spouse will feel more comfortable about the approaching interview schedule when they feel the support of both the chair and his or her spouse.

Keep in mind that during this meeting, *the candidate and his or her spouse also will be evaluating you.* If the candidate is a senior pastor candidate—will he or she want to serve under *your* district/conference leadership? If he or she is a staff candidate, this time together is even more important.

Every senior pastor knows that effective staff members are hard to find. What will attract top-quality staff prospects to join your ministry team?

Staff members agree that their most important consideration in accepting a ministry assignment is their relationship with the senior pastor.

When the staff candidate and his or her spouse meet with the senior pastor—they will be asking themselves, "Do we believe in the senior pastor's integrity? Can we count on the senior pastor's friendship and support?"

John Maxwell answers a very intriguing question on one of his Injoy Life Club tapes "What Every Staff Member Wants from Their Senior Pastor." He offers 10 "wants":

1. To be treated as a leader of value—not a hired hand
2. A commitment to open adult communication
3. Clearly understood expectations
4. To be rewarded for their work
5. Training for personal and professional growth
6. Opportunity for increasing their responsibility
7. Able to vent a disappointment and disagreement without condemnation
8. The sources needed to accomplish their work
9. His loyalty and his prayers
10. A leader with vision—not just a manager[1]

This meeting of the chair and spouse with the candidate and his or her spouse may occur before the board interview date. But if your first-time meeting is on the date of the interview, plan to meet at some private place, such as a restaurant, where you can have unhurried time to become acquainted.

After this meeting, the chair and spouse should have a few moments to themselves to ask each other these questions: "Do we sense a personal bonding with the candidate and his or her spouse?" "Would they be responsive to our leadership?" (Jesus called those who were *responsive* to Him.) "Would we enjoy having them on our team?"

CHURCH BOARD AND SPOUSES OR STAFF AND SPOUSES MEET WITH CANDIDATE AND HIS OR HER SPOUSE

The following may be an extra step in the interview process that you have not considered before. But across the years I discovered how *right* it is to include this time of fellowship.

Invite church board members and their spouses for a meal or dessert. Or if it is a staff prospect, invite the other staff members and their spouses to come for this event. Meet in a location that is conducive to "sharing." Have name tags prepared for everyone.

Remember again that the interview experience is for the candidate and his or her spouse as well as the church. The purpose of this gathering is so the candidate and his or her spouse can hear the board members or other staff introduce themselves and their spouses.

In this meeting you as the chair may mention that you will be interviewing the candidate and his or her spouse later—to learn much about *them*. Explain that *this is a time for the candidate and his or her spouse to get acquainted with other leaders*. Ask each board member or staff member to

- Introduce himself or herself, then introduce his or her spouse. If there are children living at home, he or she can share their names and ages.
- Tell about his or her ministry involvement in the church and any vocation beyond his or her church assignment.

The candidate and his or her spouse may have questions to ask some of the board or staff members and their spouses as the sharing occurs. This can be a very enjoyable time. The candidate and his or her spouse will feel more relaxed now that they have met the other leaders.

A LARGER GATHERING TO HEAR THE CHAIR INTERVIEW THE CANDIDATE AND HIS OR HER SPOUSE

If the candidate is interviewing for a staff position, the senior pastor may want to invite all the people belonging to a particular ministry group to the interview with the candidate and his or her spouse. For example, if the candidate is interviewing for youth pastor, the volunteer youth workers may be invited. If the interview is for a children's pastor, all the workers in the children's departments may be gathered together. If it's for a worship leader, perhaps everyone involved in the music ministry should be included.

If the candidate is interviewing for a senior pastorate, the district/conference leader may wish to recommend to the church board that the whole congregation be invited. The interview can be just as effective with a large gathering as with a smaller one.

In the larger gathering one suggestion is to provide seating and microphones up front for the chair, the candidate, and the spouse. Guide Sheet No. 7 has some relevant questions for the chair to ask the candidate and his or her spouse. This can be a blessed time as the candidate and his or her spouse share about their backgrounds, their family, their conversions, and so on.

At the end of the interview, you may want to ask the candidate to share a 10-minute devotional based on a scripture that has influenced his or her life and ministry. With the chair and the candidate's spouse taking a seat in the congregation, this may serve in the place of those expecting a practice sermon. It gives the congregation or group some idea of the candidate's ability to communicate. It also enables the candidate to sense the congregation's responsiveness.

If a staff prospect is being interviewed, you may want to open up the gathering so the workers in the candidate's ministry area can ask questions of the candidate and his or her spouse. This informal interaction can be both a positive experience and a chance for some personal bonding.

However, if a senior pastor is being interviewed—*as a word of caution—it is usually not wise to open this larger gathering to public questions.* One or two people with a wrong attitude can devastate the interview process. In one particular case, a negative individual upset a whole church meeting, and the candidate declined even though the board nominated him. Even if a district/conference leader has questions written out in advance and decides which ones to use, a critic may still speak out publicly if his or her questions are not addressed (if the floor is opened to questions).

As a better approach you may want to try doing this. At the end of the session with a larger group, you can state, "In a few minutes we will gather for a reception so you can personally shake hands with the candidate and his [her] spouse. If you have any questions, feel free to ask the candidate as you go through the reception line."

PLAN FOR A RECEPTION

Since people are interested in meeting the candidate and his or her spouse personally, arrange for a receiving line at the reception. A leading board member and spouse may be assigned to stand with the couple to introduce the people. Or the chair may wish to serve in that capacity.

After most of the people have passed through the receiving line, the chair should make an announcement that "the church board will be meeting with the candidate and his [her] spouse in a few minutes."

CHURCH BOARD INTERVIEW

The church board interview is the "official" interview. Refer to Guide Sheet No. 7, section E, agenda suggestions. After the chair opens with prayer, the research folders with board members' names on them should be passed out. Extra copies (without reference evaluation notes) should be given to the candidate and his or her spouse in advance.

Inform the church board that a spirit of openness is encouraged. Let them know you will welcome their questions to the candidate and his or her spouse and those from the candidate and his or her spouse to them.

You can begin by referring to the research folder sheet that summarized the three priorities agreed on from Guide Sheet 2, "Church Board Agenda: What Kind of Leader Do We Need?" The chair may wish to ask the candidate about his or her interest and experience in the first priority listed. At some point, the interaction of questions and responses will begin to "happen," with the chair taking the role of facilitator.

When the board members have had enough time to question the candidate and his or her spouse, the chair should ask the candidate, "Do you or your spouse have questions to ask the board?" Toward the end of the interaction you may want to ask the board to share their expectations of the spouse.

The chair will sense when it is the "right" time to conclude the interview. The chair may want to say something such as "In a few minutes we will dismiss the candidate and his [her] spouse. The board and I will continue the meeting. But before they leave, I know that all of us want God's will in our decisions." Ask the candidate, "Would you close in prayer, asking for God's guidance?" The candidate's prayer will often reveal his or her inner spirit. As the candidate and his or her spouse are dismissed, request that they be available nearby so that you can inform them of the board's decision.

When meeting alone with the church board, the chair may wish to share what he or she has sensed about the candidate and his or her spouse. If it is a staff member, the board will want to know the senior pastor's recommendation. Or the chair may decide to begin the meeting by asking, "What were your impressions of the candidate and his [her] spouse?"

Before voting on a candidate suggest that the board base their vote on their response to two questions:

1. **Does the candidate have the qualities and the priorities we agreed upon together?**
2. **Do you feel a personal bonding with the candidate? Would you like him or her to be your pastor/staff member?**

After open discussion together, a motion may be in order to vote on the candidate. You may want to consult your denominational bylaws at this point. They should guide you concerning voting procedures and the level of congregational involvement. For the sake of discussion, we will make certain assumptions. We will assume that the board can elect a person to a staff position without a congregational vote. But to elect a senior pastor, we will assume that the congregation has a deciding vote following the nominating vote of the board.

Before you pass out the ballots, take time again to pray, seeking God's guidance. Have board members mark their ballots. Announce the results.

If it is a vote in favor of the candidate, request that board members take a break while you convey the results of the vote to the candidate and his or her spouse. It is important to be open with the candidate as to the actual vote count. For example, rather than say, "You received the nomination or election of the board," say, "The board voted 9 to 3 in favor." The chair should offer his or her evaluation of what 9 to 3 means. In some churches, this 9 to 3 would be a divisive issue. In other situations, the 3 will cooperate fully with the majority.

When the chair informs the candidate and his or her spouse of a favorable call, the candidate and his or her spouse may request more time to pray before giving their answer. The chair should make it clear that there is no pressure to accept the board action. The candidate must receive a clear confirmation from the Lord. If the candidate is not yet sure about accepting or declining the church board action, the chair should go back to the board and report that the candidate needs more time to pray. The chair will dismiss the board and inform them later when the candidate decides to proceed or declines.

When it has been a favorable board vote, the candidate and his or her spouse may have already sensed the Holy Spirit giving them a real assurance about drawing them to this new assignment. They may feel clear on accepting the nomination or election. Suggest that they come back to the board meeting and personally tell the board of their acceptance. This can be a real time of rejoicing and praising God.

If the vote is to nominate the pastor for a congregational vote—times for announcing and holding the vote may be decided upon. If the vote was to elect a staff member, a tentative time for the staff and family to move here may be discussed.

Senior pastors and district/conference leaders, *we must remind ourselves how strongly we believe in the guidance of the Lord*. Many of us in decision making have relied on God's promise in Ps. 32:8—"I will instruct you and teach you in the way you should go; I will guide you" (NKJV).

When a district/conference leader is overseeing the call of a new senior pastor, ask the candidate to accept or decline the board's nomination *prior* to any congregational vote. Declining at this point may be disappointing to the church board, but they realize that their nomination must be confirmed in the candidate's heart. Every senior pastor candidate who agrees to proceed to a congregational vote should respond to the following question: "Will you be willing to come if the vote of the congregation is a positive one?" Candidates should be reminded that church members assume that the candidate's willingness to proceed with the congregational vote is a sign to them that the candidate would come if the vote is positive.

This does not presume that the church membership vote will always be positive. While the candidate should not expect a unanimous "yes" vote, if there is a considerable percentage of "no" votes, the candidate understandably might decline. There should be a degree of unity as a new pastor and congregation begin their partnership together.

The outline in Guide Sheet No. 7 will summarize what has been discussed in this chapter. The chair may find this a helpful resource to use throughout the process.

Throughout this interview process, *people need to be led—one step at a time.* Some chairs may not feel the need for such an extensive interview schedule. But whatever schedule you plan, remember that *taking time is important.*

It is always interesting at what point in the process the confirmation of the call, or a "red flag" blocking the confirmation, may emerge. Sometimes the sense of "knitting our hearts together" may actually occur *before* the official board meeting interview. Often the confirming of the call happens during the interview with the larger group or during the board meeting.

A note to pastors or staff being interviewed: when you accept an invitation to an interview, ask the district/conference leader or senior pastor to tell you what to expect when you arrive. If, for example, no dinner or dessert meeting is being planned with a church board or other pastoral staff before the interviews begin, you might approach the district/conference leader or senior pastor in this way, "Would it be possible for my wife [husband] and I to meet with you and the church board and spouses or pastoral staff in an informal way before we ourselves are interviewed? It would be helpful to us to get to know more about them and their ministries and involvement in the church." If you desire such a meeting, often a district/conference leader or senior pastor will be open to your suggestion.

I have often compared the coming together of a new leader with a congregation or ministry group to a marriage. When you agree to say "I do!" it is always a step of faith. But beforehand, it is important to know as much as possible about each other.

Since placing the right person in the right place should be one of our highest priorities, a thorough interview process is essential. At every point in the process, be continually reminded that you can rely on Christ's Holy Spirit to *"guide* you into all truth"* (John 16:13, emphasis added).

When the Lord confirms a call, real joy is experienced in the lives of all who are involved in the process: the chair, the candidate and his or her spouse, the board members, the staff, and the congregation. This confirmation calls for a celebration.

Celebrating the Confirmation of a Call

When I was serving as district superintendent, I interviewed an older pastor candidate and his wife in one of my churches. They informed me that in earlier days their superintendents arranged pastoral assignments simply by communicating with them over the telephone. The prospective pastor said to me, "This is the first time I've ever interviewed with a church board!"

I asked the couple, "What process did you go through when accepting a church?" The wife replied, "We just kind of *showed up!*"

Being called to a pastorate or staff position is a significant event in the life of the minister, his or her family, and the entire congregation. The results of this "marriage" will have a far-reaching influence on human lives. The arrival of a new pastor or staff member deserves more attention than just "showing up."

The installation or bonding service can be a memorable experience for the pastor, his or her family, and the entire congregation. At the end of the appendix, a sample copy of a bonding service is included. The "Service of Covenant and Commitment" is used by District Superintendent Dan Copp of the Arizona/South Nevada District Church of the Nazarene. When my present senior pastor, Craig Coulter, was installed, the whole congregation participated. It was such an uplifting time for the pastor and his family.

At the end of the "covenant," Dr. Copp asked the Coulters to come and kneel at the altar, with board members and church staff gathering around them. Dr. and Mrs. Copp prayed for them as we laid our hands upon our senior pastor and his family.

Why is it important to celebrate the confirmation of a pastoral/staff call? First, *recognition is right!* The Bible in 1 Thess. 5:12-13 instructs us to "respect those who work hard among you, who are over you in the Lord. . . . Hold them in the highest regard in love because of their work." Second, *serving the Lord and the church is the minister's life!* It means so much to the minister and family when they are appreciated.

How Do Senior Pastors Honor New Staff?

Senior pastors also celebrate the confirmation of a call to new paid staff members. What follows are examples of how several senior pastors[1] celebrate the arrival of new staff.

A pastor in Chandler, Arizona, considers this to be a significant event. He introduces the whole family publicly in his morning worship services. He then offers a commissioning prayer. After the services he plans a fellowship time in which the congregation personally greets the new staff family.

A pastor in Olathe, Kansas, introduces the new staff member and family publicly to his entire congregation. He also plans a reception when the people can greet them personally.

At a church in Denver, the pastor celebrates the arrival of staff as follows:

When new staff join our team, in our worship service we bring them to the front. I read a commitment to the staff person and spouse and have them respond publicly. I then read a commitment statement to the congregation and have them respond. Of course, it wouldn't be [complete] if we didn't pin flowers on the staff and give them a standing ovation. A reception is held following the evening service to give the congregation opportunity to greet them and eat cake.

A pastor in Lakeland, Florida, plans for this event in the following ways:

When a new staff person joins our team, we recognize the person publicly on the Sunday morning of his or her first week with us. We give gifts to the minister, spouse, and all the children. In the evening following our activities we have a special reception for the new staff member and his or her family.

A Bethany, Oklahoma, pastor uses the following procedure in recognizing his new arrivals:

- Photographs and news releases in church publications.
- A luncheon with staff in which they are introduced and welcomed.
- A commissioning time in all three morning services in which the staff person and family are presented. Other staff and key leaders gather to lay on hands and consecrate their ministry.
- A reception that may involve the entire church if the particular ministry impacts the whole church, or if a particular age group—parents and/or other appropriate people.

Whether we are welcoming a new senior pastor or a staff member, we should take time to praise God for the culmination of a process. There has been much prayer, time, and energy spent by the caller, the church board, and the candidate. The new leader is entering a brand-new chapter of his or her life. The leader and family have left close relationships with friends in a previous assignment. Major adjustments will be facing each family member.

One of the hardest things ministers and their families experience is being taken for granted. This bonding or installation service lets the newcomers know they are valued and loved.

It would make interesting reading if we could record the comments of ministers, spouses, and their children after they have experienced their first Sunday in a new church. I remember driving to the parsonage after our first service in our third pastorate. We had just experienced a wonderful welcoming service. I asked my family, "How do you feel about our new church?" Dave replied, "I like it!" Dan said, "I think they really are accepting us!" Judi responded, "My Sunday School teacher cares about me!" My wife summarized our sentiments very clearly: "I feel like kicking off my shoes. I'm home!"

9

Fulfillment from Choosing Effective Leaders

An article in our denomination's monthly magazine caught my attention. It was a tribute to a man who had profoundly influenced Gary, the writer of the article.

I was serving as youth pastor of a Kansas City church during my seminary years. I realized that in building a dynamic youth group, a good place to start was reaching fifth and sixth graders. So when I organized junior and senior high basketball teams, I also started a team for preteens. That's when I met Gary.

Gary was short for his age but had a real enthusiasm for playing on the team. His father and mother were divorced. Gary lived with his mom, who was doing all she could to keep Gary involved at church.

Gary and the other preteen boys started bringing their friends to join the team. There were too many for me to transport in the church van. I needed help. That's when Jim Spruill came into the picture.

My first memory of getting to know Jim was in the church foyer. After the morning service he had stopped to chat with Gary and two other boys. When I saw his interest in kids, I went to Jim, introduced myself, and said, "Would you be willing to drive your car next Saturday to help me haul these kids to basketball practice?" Without hesitation Jim agreed.

Jim formed a bond of friendship with those boys—especially Gary. Jim had two boys of his own, and Gary became like his oldest son. Jim and his wife, Pauline, consented to becoming my junior high directors when Gary moved up to seventh grade.

I had no idea of the impact Jim was having on Gary's life until I read the magazine article. Gary—Gary Sivewright—is now chaplain of Mount Vernon Nazarene University in Mount Vernon, Ohio. He speaks to young people around the world.

Gary wrote me recently and shared the following words about Jim Spruill's influence:

> Jim was always there for me during those years. Whenever I needed a ride to church, Jim was there. He was a shy man . . . very uncomfortable when speaking. He never preached a sermon. But I am convinced that because of Jim Spruill's love for me and his investment in my life, I'm in the church today—preaching, writing and teaching.[1]

When I reflected on having a part in recruiting Jim, I began to rejoice in the Lord. Talk about fulfillment! This still moves me with a deep sense of gratitude to God.

I believe the greatest joy in life is to personally receive Christ as Savior. The next greatest fulfillment comes when we influence someone else to become a Christian or when we choose a leader whom God uses to win others to Christ.

If you are a district/conference leader, a senior pastor, or a staff member, you know how fulfilling it is to select the right leaders for ministry assignments. To see the impact of leader's lives upon others makes all the time spent in the process of their selection worthwhile.

We who are called to choose effective leaders have to face the painful reality that sometimes we do make the wrong choices. It may bring some comfort to know that even Jesus was not able to get all 12 disciples to follow His leadership. Judas Iscariot was not only a bitter disappointment to Jesus but also brought turmoil into Christ's leadership team.

The apostle Paul also experienced the anguish of failure. In Paul's final letter, 2 Timothy, he was writing from a Roman prison, recalling the names of his many leaders who were serving throughout the civilized world. In 2 Tim. 4:10, Paul writes that "Demas, because he loved this world, has deserted me and has gone to Thessalonica." Who was Demas? In Philem. 24, Paul includes Demas as one of "my fellow workers." Demas was a leader who failed in the ministry.

It may offer us some consolation to remember that *both* Jesus and the apostle Paul chose a team member who left the ministry. As I reflect on my own years in church leadership, I can truthfully make the following statement: *Across the years, the deepest heartaches that I experienced came from my choosing the wrong persons for leadership positions.*

Some whom I selected developed bad attitudes *after* they came to their new assignments. Their problems were difficult to identify beforehand—even with the use of a very careful process. But there were other leaders I should have researched more thoroughly. Under the pressure of time, I moved ahead too quickly.

I remember a new convert in my first church whom I placed in a position of lay leadership. He became proud of his new authority and increasingly critical of anyone who crossed him. In this case I had not heeded the biblical warning: "He must not be a recent convert, or he may become conceited" (1 Tim. 3:6).

A youth pastor in one of my pastorates had to be replaced. He came to the teen meetings unprepared and was not open to any of my suggestions. The group declined numerically and in morale. It became an ordeal before we could finally remove him.

As a district superintendent, I once worked with a board in one of my stronger churches to call a senior pastor. The leading candidate had been pastoring a church on another district. I checked out two references who gave favorable reports. Somehow I had neglected to ask any questions on how he dealt with conflict. Soon after he came to his new assignment, it was evident that things were not going well. When I tried to offer help, he reacted angrily. When he finally agreed to leave, the church was about one half its former size.

Sometime later, a man who had known him previously said to me, "I wish you had checked with me before you called him. I had several volatile encounters with him, and I could have warned you." Following this man's comment, I vowed I would henceforth seek out more objective references and do a better job of calling leaders. Unwise choices have far-reaching consequences.

Looking back over my lifetime of choosing leaders, I don't dwell on the few wrong choices. Rather, I experience the deep fulfillment that comes from selecting the many "right" leaders who have been effective in building Christ's kingdom.

There is the fulfillment that comes from friendship with wisely chosen leaders. Senior pastors and district/conference leaders who are responsible for choosing staff and pastors can relate to the closeness that Jesus felt to His disciples. We identify with Christ's desire to be with them at His last meal. His love is evident in His words: "I have eagerly desired to eat this Passover with you" (Luke 22:15).

Paul, like Jesus, cherished his friendships. At the end of his life, he closes his writing with personal remarks. He begins by telling of Demas, who deserted him, but then writes about two friends who were to influence the whole world as Gospel writers. Paul says, "Only Luke is with me." And he asks for Mark. Mark had earlier dropped out of the ministry, but now Paul tells Timothy to "Get Mark and bring him with you, because he is helpful to me in my ministry" (2 Tim. 4:11).

When people ask me if I miss being a senior pastor or a district superintendent, my response is, "No—but I do miss the friendships with pastors, associates, and lay leaders." When you pray and plan together and overcome the many challenges that confront the ministry—there is a partnership bond that is deep and lasting.

I recall meeting with seven members of a church. The total attendance was down to about 15. Their pastor had resigned. I anticipated that they might want to close the church. But when I met with them, they were not discouraged. They said to me, "We believe that God can still use us to build a strong Holiness church in our community. Find us a good pastor, and we will work with him!"

I did find a pastor who felt he had four years left before retirement. He and his wife were strong, caring leaders. People were drawn to Christ through their outreach and love. Four years later when he resigned, we had a healthy, positive congregation averaging 50 in attendance.

When I started working with the church board to find a replacement, I thought of a man on my district who had been saved out of the drug culture. He and his wife's lives had been wonderfully transformed. His pastor saw the potential in him and asked him to teach an adult Sunday School class. I began to hear news of people being saved and his class showing remarkable growth. Then the pastor told me that God had called this young man to preach. The pastor opened his pulpit for him to preach on Sunday nights once a month, and new people were accepting Christ. One year later this "Kingdom-minded" pastor phoned me and said, "I'd like to keep him here in my church, but he's really ready to pastor!"

The Lord clearly led this young man to interview and accept this new assignment. Under his leadership the congregation of 50 grew to 100. He found it necessary to start double worship services. Then his church purchased seven acres of land in the growing section of the community. That church, which had been down to a small nucleus, now has three morning worship services and is averaging 300 in attendance.

As I reflect on what has happened, my spirit soars in thankfulness to God. I thank Him for seven faithful board members and a pastor who gave four years before retirement. Oh, the gratitude I feel for that mentoring pastor who nurtured this young leader—and finally for God's guiding me to this effective pastor. He and his people are impacting their entire community for Christ.

When a pastor grows a church, a youth pastor builds a dynamic teen group, a children's pastor recruits a team of effective teachers, or a minister of music develops inspiring praise and worship— the one who called these leaders will experience real fulfillment. There are also gratifying rewards when the right leaders are called to deal with difficult situations.

I once placed a pastor in a midsize church on my district. Within a year he phoned me with the shocking news of a moral failure by his associate pastor. The man had been on staff there prior to the new pastor's coming. The staff man was very gifted and well liked by the new pastor and the people. Then the news broke of his sexual unfaithfulness with several persons in a city 40 miles away.

The church began to polarize over how to deal with the man.

Some started blaming his wife and children. Others wanted to overlook the associate's sin and keep him on staff. But the senior pastor dealt with this hostile congregation with unusual wisdom. He secured the resignation from the man. He recommended to his church board that they continue financial support for the man's wife and family. His calm leadership decisions eventually brought that church through the crisis.

As I remember the many leaders that God guided me to call to ministry assignments, this wise pastor is near the top of my list. He suffered through the conflict and saved the church. Today that church is a strong, growing congregation—one of the largest in the community. Whenever I hear of the great things now happening in this church—I think of this former pastor. I will forever give praise to God for His guidance in leading me to call him there.

Someday when we stand before God, the most anticipated words that we could ever hope to hear will be "Well done, good and faithful servant. . . . Enter into the joy of your lord" (Matt. 25:21, NKJV). When we get to heaven, the greatest joy will surely be the presence of Jesus himself. German pastor Helmut Thielicke clearly describes this truth:

> Heaven does not consist in what we shall receive, whether this be white robes and heavenly crowns . . . but rather in what we shall become—namely, the companions of our King, who then will always be able to see Him and be near to Him as to a brother, no longer seeing through a glass darkly . . . but praising God with never a tear in our eyes.[2]

We will also experience the delight of being reunited with loved ones who preceded us and those who follow us to heaven. Then how marvelous will be the time we spend with those we have personally influenced to accept Christ as their Savior! We will rejoice over having been one of the Spirit's channels to lead the lost to Christ.

I believe that heaven will be a place of eternal surprises. Among the surprises that I envision will be hearing of those who came to Jesus, not through our direct influence but rather through the lives of the leaders we called.

Just think about listening to people's testimonies of how they came out of the bondage of sin because some leaders had loved them to Christ. What gladness it will bring when we discover that the leaders mentioned were among those God had led us to place in leadership positions!

Staying close enough to Christ's guiding Spirit so that we build a great team will always be a challenge. But, oh, the fulfillment we will experience here on earth—and eternally in heaven!

Appendix

Guide Sheet No. 1*
Church Board Agendas for Calling
a Pastor or Paid Staff Member

A special church board meeting should be scheduled within a few days after a pastor or staff resignation.

SUGGESTED AGENDA

- Inform the church board that you will be working closely with them.
- Decide together on how to bring a good closure for outgoing pastor or staff (plans for farewell, financial considerations, and so on).
- Discuss interim arrangements.
- Give a brief overview of the process of calling another leader.

Church Board Meeting
After the Resigning Leader Has Moved Away

Devotional: Eph. 4:11-13—How Christ builds up the Body

SUGGESTED AGENDA

A. Convey to the board that while you as chair will be making the contact with candidates, that *the choosing of leaders is to be a shared responsibility.* Present four principles to be discussed and agreed upon:

---

*Permission is granted upon purchase to copy these guide sheets for noncommercial use.

1. The Holy Spirit leads board members as well as the chair.
2. Clarify the roles and procedures in the calling of a leader. Consult your denomination's bylaws for specific procedures and protocols for calling senior pastors and paid staff.
3. Every board member's viewpoint is important.
4. Express your viewpoint *in* the board meetings—not outside the meetings. Speak and vote individually rather than by groups.

Suggest to the board that before we talk about *who* we can call we consider two important questions:

1. Where are we as a church—now? Let's look at our strengths and concerns.
2. What kind of leader do we need?

B. Where are we as a church? The church is called a "body." It is alive, and it changes. How would you describe our church body? "Church" refers to our *people* and also a *place.*

1. What are our strengths?

   a. *What are the positive qualities about our people? Are we friendly? Do new people express that they feel accepted?*

   _____

   _____

   b. *What are the good things about our place—our community, buildings, location, finances, and so on?*

   _____

   _____

2. What are concerns about our church? What attitudes do we need to face and address as a *people?*

   _____

   Is there a concern that should be addressed during the interim?

   _____

   _____

Are there concerns about our *place*—facility limitations and so on?

_____

_____

C. If you are considering hiring paid staff—what are the positive strengths in the specific area of ministry to be filled?

_____

_____

What realities and challenges will he or she face?

_____

_____

Chair: Is there any problem that should be dealt with now? Don't leave it for the new staff person to deal with!

_____

_____

(Note: you may decide to proceed on to Guide Sheet No. 2. Or you may want to schedule another meeting to discuss "What kind of leader do we need?")

Guide Sheet No. 2
Church Board Agenda:
What Kind of Leader Do We Need?

Devotional: 1 Tim. 3:1-6—The qualities of a leader

A. Primary roles of a pastor/staff member
   1. A clear call to ministry
   2. Committed to being a person of prayer
   3. Effective in his or her area of ministry
   4. Possessing the basic attributes of character

B. If you are a senior pastor considering a paid staff member, you may want to adapt this list to other primary roles desired.

   ___ Preacher/Teacher of the Word—applies the Bible to our lives.

   ___ Administrator/Equipper—sets vision and goals. Recruits workers and equips them for ministry.

   ___ Relates well to people—is supportive of others on the team.

   ___ Evangelist—effective in reaching new people and leading them to Christ.

   ___ Counselor—helping people face life; a good listener.

   1. Discuss together, "How important is being an effective preacher/teacher to your church at this time? How important is being an effective administrator/equipper?" and so on.
   2. Ask board members to each write in a vertical column the numbers 1 to 5. Then request that they place next to no. 1 the role that is *most* important to them. No. 2 is second most important, and so on. Tell them to be sure to fill in all five.
   3. Ask someone to tabulate the numbers as you call for "preacher/teacher." Have the tabulator write down each number expressed around the circle for each role. When the tabulator adds totals, the role with lowest combined total will be no. 1—the highest priority. The next lowest total will be no. 2, and so on.

Convey to the board that when you start contacting prospects and references, you will focus on the top three roles that have been identified.

C. Are there other qualities you regard as important in your next pastor or staff member? Refer to the section in this book titled "What Senior Pastors Look For in Prospective Staff."

_____

_____

D. What will your expectations of a leader's spouse be? (Remind the board that the spouse will be *different* from former ministers' spouses.)

_____

_____

E. Decide on financial support to be offered to the pastor or staff. (Refer to the explanation in this book that the minister's compensation is *different* from that of an employee in a business.)

Keep both faith and reality in mind.

$_____ Housing/Utility allowance

_____ Social Security

_____ Salary

_____ Tax-sheltered annuity

$_____ Total monthly

Expenses not included in usual employee compensation:

$_____ Auto reimbursement

_____ Medical/Dental insurance

$_____ Total monthly

F. If you're ready to proceed, first read the background information from the opening paragraphs of chapter 4. Then receive names of prospects from the church board. Add the prospect names you are wanting to include. Remind the board at this point *not* to promote one prospect over another. Let the board know that you will do research on prospects and contact each one to find out if he or she is open to being considered. If it is premature to receive prospect names now, let the board members know that this may occur at the next board meeting.

Guide Sheet No. 3
Prospect Information

Name of prospect _____

Church where presently serving _____

District _____

Before phoning prospect, secure the following information from your church's local or national/international headquarters:

Spouse's name _____

Home phone number (___)_____

Date prospect began ministry there _____
   (This may not be available for a staff member.)

1. CHURCH/MINISTRY INFORMATION
   Members joining by profession of faith this year _____
   Previous year _____
   People growth (Compare figures of first year to those of present year.)   Membership   A.M. worship   S.S. attend.
         ( ) ( )   ( ) ( )   ( ) ( )
   Financial Review
   Raised in the church for all purposes: $_____ $_____
   Cash salary: $_____ $_____
   Employee benefits: $_____ $_____

2. IF A PROSPECT FOR STAFF POSITION
   People growth (Compare figures of first year to those of present year.)   Children S.S. attend.   Youth S.S. attend.
       ( ) ( )   ( ) ( )
   Financial Review
   Associate Salary $_____ $_____
   Assoc. employee benefits: $_____ $_____

3. IF PROSPECT IS COMING FROM A COLLEGE OR SEMINARY WITH NO PREVIOUS ENTRIES IN DENOMINATIONAL RECORDS:

Find out where prospect attended church while a student. Did he or she serve in some capacity in the local church? Ask for

Church attended _____

District _____

Senior pastor's name _____

Church phone (___)_____

Home phone (___)_____

After receiving the pastor's evaluation of the student prospect, ask pastor for the names of other objective references—those who worked with the prospect in the local church:

Names _____ Phone (___)_____

_____ Phone (___)_____

Guide Sheet No. 4
Initial Phone Conversation
with Prospect

Name _____ Present location _____

Home phone (___)_____

Before phoning, offer your prayer to God asking for the Holy Spirit's guidance.

Keeping Guide Sheet No. 3 before you will provide some background information.

1. Introduce yourself.

2. Say something like "Your name has been suggested as a possible prospect for _____. Would you be open to hearing more about this?" If his or her answer is "No," let the prospect know that you understand and may contact him or her sometime in the future.

3. If his or her answer is "Yes—I'm interested in hearing about this," then proceed. Describe your open position. Share the church board's and your evaluation about the church, and also what qualities they needed in a pastor. (Refer to Guide Sheets No. 1 and No. 2.) Inform the prospect of the financial support offered. Be specific about housing, medical insurance, social security, and so on. Conclude with *your* realistic assessment of the church or staff position and the potential you envision.

4. Then ask, "After hearing about this opening, would you allow your name to be considered along with other interested candidates at our next board meeting?" _____

5. If "Yes," proceed with some of the following questions:

Do you have children still at home? _____ Names and

grades: _____

_____

When you came to your present assignment, what goals did you hope to achieve? _____

_____

_____

What goals did the Lord enable you to accomplish? _____

_____

_____

Which goals did not become a reality? _____

_____

_____

What do you like most about your current assignment? _____

_____

What do you like least about your current assignment?

_____

_____

6. Possible references (*not* those presently attending his or her church):

> Ask, "Are there any persons who served with you in a previous assignment who would be objective in their evaluation of your ministry?" Or "Are there any who have moved away from where you are now assigned who would be objective references?"
>
> Name _____
>
> Leadership position _____
>
> "How long did he [she] serve with you?"_____
>
> Would you have a phone number? (___)_____
>
> Name _____

Leadership position _____

"How long did he [she] serve with you?"_____

Would you have a phone number? (___)_____

7. Let the prospect know that you realize that this is just a step in the process, but you may include his or her name with other prospects in the next church board meeting. If the board desires to request more information—you will be back in contact with him or her. Thank the prospect for his or her time and openness.

Guide Sheet No. 5
An Evaluation by a Reference

Take time for prayer to ask God for discernment before you begin making phone calls. Be sensitive to the Holy Spirit's leading in your interaction with the reference.

Name of reference _____ Phone (___)_____

I. INTRODUCTORY REMARKS TO A REFERENCE

"My name is _____. I am _____
(pastor, district/conference leader)

of _____. _____

(church/district)   (candidate's name)

has been suggested to me as a possible candidate as a _____

_____. You're aware of how impor-

(pastor/youth pastor/children's pastor, or so on)

tant it is to call the right person to the right place. You had been referred to me as a person who has known the candidate or served with him [her]. If I were to keep your name confidential, would you be willing to answer some questions?" If "Yes," then proceed.

Remember when asking questions:
The best predictor of future behavior
is past behavior.

II. INFORMATION ABOUT THE REFERENCE

Where was the minister serving when you became acquainted? _____ In what position did he [she] serve? _____ What was your position when you knew or worked with him [her]? _____

III. QUESTIONS TO ASK THE REFERENCE (Note: You may decide to skip some of the following questions that may not apply to the candidate.)

1. If the candidate was married when he [she] was known by the reference:
   - Would you consider that he [she] had a strong marriage?

   _____

   In what ways was this evident to you? _____

   _____

   - If there are children in the house, have the parents raised them with both love and discipline? _____

2. What would you say were his [her] greatest strengths?

   _____

   _____

3. If you were to name an area in which he [she] needs to grow, what would it be? _____

   _____

4. In regard to preaching/teaching ability:
   - Did he [she] use the Bible effectively? ( ) yes ( ) somewhat ( ) no
   - Was he [she] interesting? ( ) yes ( ) average ( ) no
   - Did you grow spiritually through his [her] ministry? _____ In what way? _____

   _____

5. Was relating to people one of his [her] strengths?
   - Can you think of an example? _____
   - How did he [she] deal with opposition or conflict? _____ An example: _____

   _____

   - When he [she] may not agree with a decision by the church board or pastor, will he [she] still support and be a team player? _____ Can you think of an example?

   _____

   _____

6. Was he [she] willing to be accountable to whom he [she] was responsible (church board, senior pastor)? _____ An example: _____

   _____

7. Was candidate effective in winning the unsaved?
   - Do you know of those whom he [she] influenced for Christ? _____

8. In regard to his [her] administrative ability:
   - Did he [she] have a vision for what needed to be accomplished? _____ Are you aware that some of his [her] vision actually happened? Describe it. _____

     _____

   - Was he [she] open to the input of others? _____ Can you think of an example? _____

     _____

   - How effective was he [she] in delegating tasks to others? An example? _____

     _____

   - Was he [she] good on follow-through of plans? _____ Can you think of an event that illustrates this? _____

     _____

     _____

   - Was he [she] able to recruit workers effectively? _____ Do you know of someone who worked with him [her] in ministry? _____ Was he [she] positive about the candidate's leadership? _____ Would this person be a good reference? _____ Name _____ Do you know his [her] phone number? (___)_____

9. Suppose that you were to move away from where you now live, and you found that the candidate was pastor/staff member of a nearby church. Would you be enthusiastic about attending there? _____

10. Are there any other observations that you would want to add about this candidate? _____

    _____

Thank you for your time. We do want God's will for this church and this candidate.

Guide Sheet No. 6
Preparation for Church Board Meeting
and Suggested Agenda

(Note: It will be helpful to read through chapter 6 for the reasons supporting these guidelines.)

I. PREPARATION BY THE CHAIR PRIOR TO THE BOARD MEETING

   1. Arrange a meeting when all board members will be present.
   2. Prepare a folder for each board member. (Refer to this guide sheet for a description of what information to include.)
   3. Organize your reference evaluations—read through and project apparent serious candidates.
   4. Contact the two or three whom you consider to be serious candidates. Ask if they are open to a possible interview. Inquire of several tentative dates that they might come— should the board vote to call them for an interview.

II. REVIEWING EVALUATIONS—SUGGESTED BOARD AGENDA

   Devotional: Read Acts 16:1-3. Paul offers us a biblical pattern for choosing a leader: (1) Paul inquired of Timothy's background, (2) he checked references in two churches where Timothy had served, and (3) he met him personally—the reason for an interview. (Refer to "The Early Church Pattern" section near the beginning of chapter 5.) Take time to pray together.

   A. Clarify some guidelines as to how you will proceed together.

      1. *Recommend that the board interview candidates one at a time* rather than meeting two or more and then deciding between them. Explain your rationale (refer to chapter 6).
      2. *Agree together that the spouse of the candidate also be asked to be present for the interview.* Both the spouse and

the board need this time together in order for such an important decision to be made.

3. *Communicate that neither the candidate nor the board are obligated to approve or accept a nomination.* The interview does indicate a *real interest* in taking this step in the process.

B. Review evaluations of references with the board.

1. Pass out folders to each board member. Ask them to write their name on the folder. Mention to them that this folder will be passed out to them again when an interview occurs.

2. On the first sheet of their folder read through the list of names of the prospects who declined consideration.

3. On the second sheet list the top three qualities or roles that they decided were important when they considered "What Kind of Leader Do We Need?" (Guide Sheet No. 2). Request that they listen for these qualities as you read reference evaluations. Suggest that they take notes.

4. Inform the board that you will proceed by reading through the information in their folder three times:
   - First, the personal background on each candidate (printed from Guide Sheet No. 3).
   - The second time through, share the responses by the candidates themselves to your questions (your reading from Guide Sheet No. 4).
   - Finally, you will read the evaluations by the objective references you contacted (Guide Sheet No. 5).

5. Before you read to the board the reference evaluations, state that you are keeping their *names* of references confidential. You *will* reveal the association of the reference to the candidate and how long the reference has known him or her.

C. Condense the list to serious candidates.

1. After reading through the background and evaluations

to the board, ask, "Are there comments or questions that you have about a candidate?"

2. *Note at this point*—offer any of your personal observations on particular candidates. It may be clear that the board would be open to your suggestions related to the following:

a. Reduce the number of serious candidates for an interview to two or three. If this is their desire, distribute ballots. Request that they keep in mind which candidates have the qualities they need. Pause for a prayer for God's guidance. Ask them to write two or three names. Have the board secretary and a board member next to the secretary compile the results together. Go back and review evaluations on the two or three. Distribute another ballot. Ask them to write the name of the one candidate that they desire to interview. Or—

b. It may be clear to the board and the chair that one candidate is clearly the desired person to call for an interview. Often this may be the case when a senior pastor is recommending a staff member. A vote by ballot may be in order.

D. Confirm the interview.

1. Suggest two possible dates for an interview that would coincide with the candidate's available dates. Make sure that all (or nearly all) board members could be present on date that's favored for the interview.

2. Ask the board to take a break while you phone the candidate. Confirm the date that would be best for the board and the candidate and his or her spouse to come for an interview. Report the candidate's confirmation back to board.

E. Make preliminary plans for the interview schedule with the candidate and his or her spouse. (Refer to chapter 7 for reasons supporting these gatherings.) The chair will want to spend personal time alone with candidate and his or her spouse prior to the following meeting times. Adapt the schedule to whatever seems best for your situation. Inform the board of the projected schedule so they will know when to be present.

- Suggest that it is helpful to begin the process with a *friendship time for chair, candidate, and spouse with board or other pastoral staff and spouses*—perhaps a meal or dessert time together. (Set time and place.) _____

- *Plan to meet with a larger group* (congregation meet with pastor candidate, or if staff member, with their ministry group). Refer to comments expressed in chapter 7. This larger group will appreciate hearing the chairman interview the candidate and his or her spouse—their testimonies, candidate's call to ministry, and so on. (Also set time and place.) _____

- *Arrange for a reception* when people can personally meet the candidate and his or her spouse.

- Meet for the *official interview by church board with chair, candidate, and spouse.* This should be a time of open interaction together. At the end, the chair will dismiss the candidate and his or her spouse. The chair and board will discuss the interview. The board may or may not choose to nominate the pastor candidate or elect a staff member.

Note to chair: After the board meeting or the next day, notify the other serious candidates whom you phoned about a possible interview. Out of consideration for them, bring them up to date on the action of the board to interview another candidate. Let them know that if the first candidate is not chosen, you may be in touch with them again. They will appreciate your keeping them informed. It will also let them know that you are interested in *them,* and not just in filling a position.

Guide Sheet No. 7
The Process of Interviewing

(Note: You may wish to refer to chapter 7 for other information.)

The purpose of the interview is to give an opportunity for the chair, candidate and his or her spouse, and the church leaders and members to *become personally acquainted with each other.* A suggested schedule is as follows:

A. THE CHAIR MEETS WITH THE CANDIDATE AND HIS OR HER SPOUSE before interview meetings begin. If possible, the chair's spouse should also be included. (Refer to chapter 7 for suggestions about this meeting.) Set time and place: _____

B. THE CANDIDATE AND HIS OR HER SPOUSE WITH THE CHAIR MEET THE CHURCH BOARD MEMBERS OR THE PASTORAL STAFF AND THEIR SPOUSES. Often this can be a meal or dessert time together. The main purpose here is for the candidate and his or her spouse to get acquainted with other local leaders and their spouses. The chair may ask board members or pastoral staff and spouses to share with the candidate: their name and spouse's name, their vocation, and their ministry in the church. Have name tags for everyone present. Set time and place: _____

C. A LARGER GATHERING TO HEAR THE CHAIR INTERVIEW THE CANDIDATE AND HIS OR HER SPOUSE. If the position open is for a senior pastor, the whole congregation may be invited. If the job opening is for a staff member, the candidate should meet with those whom he or she would be working in a ministry area. (Refer to chapter 7 for explanation.)
   1. Set time and place _____ for chairman to interview the candidate and his or her spouse.
   2. Some suggested questions for chair to ask the candidate and his or her spouse:

- Where were you born and raised?
- Describe the spiritual influences on your life.
- How and when were you saved?
- What led to your making the deeper commitment to be filled with the Holy Spirit?
- (Candidate only) Tell about your call to the ministry.
- (If married) How did you meet each other?
- What was there about her [him] that influenced you to make her [him] your life companion?
- (If they have children) Tell about your children's names, their ages, and their interests.
- Where have you served in ministry?
- What has been most fulfilling to you in your present assignment?
- What has led you to take this step in coming here for an interview?
- Other pertinent questions: _____

_____

_____

_____

_____

3. At the end of the interview, ask the candidate to speak briefly about a Bible passage that God has used to influence his or her life. The candidate's sharing will give the audience some exposure on how the candidate communicates. Also, the candidate can sense the responsiveness to his or her sharing.

4. At the end of this session, the chair may invite people to a reception where they can meet the candidate and his or her spouse personally. Mention, "If any of you have questions, feel free to ask the candidate when you introduce yourself at the reception." (Note: A caution against opening up to questions in the larger group. Refer to reasons explained in chapter 7.) Inform the people that after the reception when

they have met the candidate and his or her spouse, you and the church board will be meeting with the candidate and his or her spouse. Close with prayer (and offer grace if food will be served).

D. RECEPTION for people to meet candidate and his or her spouse in a receiving line.

E. CHURCH BOARD INTERVIEW AGENDA

1. Arrange seats in a way that encourages interaction. Chair opens with prayer. Suggest that here will be ample opportunity for the board members to ask the candidate and his or her spouse questions, and in turn for the candidate and his or her spouse to ask questions of the church board. Encourage an atmosphere of openness as you seek God's will together. Distribute to the board their research folders with the candidate's background page, summary of "What Kind of Leader Do We Need?" and reference evaluations. (Remove other candidate sheets and all other candidate reference evaluations beforehand.)

    A good way to begin is to refer to three top roles or priorities on the page: "What Kind of Leader Do We Need?" If the top priority is "Preacher/Teacher," the chair might ask, "How do you prepare for preaching/teaching? What time investment do you make each week, and when do you study? What do you hope to accomplish when you speak?" Such questions can get the discussion started. Suggest that board members should feel free to ask questions about this and other priorities. The chair may ask a pertinent question: "What expectations do you have of the pastor's/staff member's spouse?"

    After board members have had ample opportunity to ask questions, suggest to the candidate and his or her spouse, "You may have questions to ask the board." After the interaction slows down, the chair may *ask the candidate to close in prayer* that God will guide in the decision. Then excuse the candidate and his or her spouse. As they are leaving, let them know that they should be available for you to convey to them the church board's decision.

2. *Chair and church board meet together.* The chair asks the board of their impression of the candidate and his or her spouse. After discussion, the board may or may not decide to nominate the candidate for a vote to the congregation. If this is a staff position, does the chairman/pastor offer a nomination that the board elect him or her? The chair may pass out ballots and say, "Before we pray, I would suggest that your vote "for" or "against" based on two considerations:

   a. "Does the candidate have the primary qualities that you desired in 'What kind of leader?'"

   b. On the personal level, "Would you like this candidate to be your pastor or on your pastoral team?"

   Chair or board members pray for God's guidance. Then ask them to cast their votes and pass the ballots to you and the board secretary. Announce the vote. Inform the board that you will convey the vote to the candidate. Request that the board members stay until the chair reports back to the board that the candidate requests more time to pray. Or if candidate and his or her spouse feel confirmed to accept, the chair may suggest that they return to the board to personally express their acceptance. If a pastor candidate, set times to announce the vote by the church membership. If a staff candidate, a tentative time may even be suggested as to when they could move here.

Plan to celebrate their coming. Refer to chapter 8, "Celebrating the Confirmation of a Call."

A Service of Covenant and Commitment

DISTRICT/CONFERENCE LEADER

One very special relationship is that of a people with their pastor. Our Lord pictured this relationship, with its warmth and meaning, in the imagery of a shepherd and his sheep. People of the congregation at [insert church name], what covenant and commitment do you make with your new pastor, [insert name]?

CONGREGATION

Before God, we covenant to pray for you as our leader, shepherd, and pastor. Bonding at its most meaningful level happens as we celebrate, grieve, laugh, weep, dream, and achieve together. We already love you. That love will grow and deepen and will never end.

DISTRICT/CONFERENCE LEADER

As pastor, [insert name] is called to an important role of leadership among you. What covenants and commitments do you make as you partner in ministry with your pastor?

CONGREGATION

Pastor, we want you to share with us the vision God gives you for this church family. We promise to dream, think, and pray with you for God's plan for our church. We will respect each other's opinions and ideas. We will seek God's direction in all things so we can come together to say, "It seems good to the Holy Spirit and to us."

PASTOR

God has called me to this church, and I will establish my ministry upon the Word of God. As your pastor, I intend to continue my personal growth in Jesus Christ.

- I will be honest with the use of my time.

- I will be fair with my family—placing high priority on their needs.
- I will handle responsibly all confidences shared with me.
- I will seek to use my gifts in developing and equipping you for works of ministry.
- I will strive to remain receptive to suggestions intended to strengthen our ministry together.
- I will exercise the necessary discipline to stay mentally, spiritually, and physically fit.
- I will be honest in my stewardship of the resources God has entrusted to me.
- I will guard the integrity of our church and myself.

DISTRICT/CONFERENCE LEADER

People, what covenant do you make with [insert names of pastor's family members]?

CONGREGATION

[Insert name of pastor's spouse], we welcome you to our church family. We commit to accept you and pray for you as a woman [man], a wife [husband], and a person with individual value who is an important part of the team. We open our hearts and offer our love to you.

[Insert name(s) of pastor's children], we welcome you to our church family. You are young people created in the image of God, and He has a unique place for you. We want [insert name of church] to be a place where you will each grow to be like Jesus. We open our hearts and offer our love to you.

DISTRICT/CONFERENCE LEADER

[Insert names of pastor and spouse], what covenants and commitments do you make with your church family?

PASTOR AND SPOUSE

We offer ourselves to you now without reservation. As our

church family we will love, trust, believe, and honor you. We will treat you as individuals each with worth and importance.

By His grace we will lovingly accept each other's strengths and weaknesses.

CONGREGATION

We accept your love. We accept *you*. Today we begin together.

ALL TOGETHER

Today we begin a journey together that will be good and long, a journey that will lead to a deepening love for Christ and each other and a redemptive mission to our world.

May His
grace and presence
be ours
_____ *for the journey*

Adapted from Dan Copp, "A Service of Covenant and Commitment," Arizona-S. Nevada District Church of the Nazarene, 2001.

Notes

Introduction

1. Jim Collins, *Good to Great* (New York: HarperBusiness, 2001), 13.

Chapter 1

1. George Barna, *Boiling Point—Monitoring Cultural Shifts in the 21st Century* (Ventura, Calif.: Regal Books, 2001), 94-95.

2. Dale Galloway, *Building Teams in Ministry* (Kansas City: Beacon Hill Press of Kansas City, 2001), 95.

3. Josh McDowell, "The Contagious Evangelist," *Christianity Today,* October 2003, 53.

4. James Dobson, *Bringing Up Boys* (Wheaton, Ill.: Tyndale House, 2001), 246.

5. Dan Spaite, *Time Bomb in the Church—Defusing Pastoral Burnout* (Kansas City: Beacon Hill Press of Kansas City, 1999), 164-65.

6. James S. Stewart, *The Life and Teaching of Jesus Christ* (New York: Abingdon Press), 101.

7. Ronnie W. Floyd, *How to Pray* (Nashville: Word, 1999), 79.

8. Alan Loy McGinnis, *The Friendship Factor* (Minneapolis: Augsburg Press, 1979), 15.

9. Charles Osborne, *The Art of Getting Along with People* (Grand Rapids: Zondervan Publishing House, 1980), 49.

10. Galloway, *Building Teams in Ministry,* 23.

11. The five pastors include No. 1, J. K. Warrick of College Church of the Nazarene, Olathe, Kans.; No. 2, Mark Fuller of Crossroads Church of the Nazarene, Chandler, Ariz.; No. 3, Tim Stearman of First Church of the Nazarene, Denver; No. 4, Larry Leonard of Highland Park Church of the Nazarene, Lakeland, Fla.; and No. 5, Mel McCullough of First Church of the Nazarene, Bethany, Okla.

12. Collins, *Good to Great,* 51.

Chapter 2

1. Charles Ridley, District Superintendents' Leaders Conference, Dallas, September 24, 1991.

Chapter 3

1. Stan Toler, *Church Operations Manual—A Step-by-Step Guide to Effective Church Management* (Kansas City: Beacon Hill Press of Kansas City, 2001), 18-36.

Chapter 4

1. Galloway, *Building Teams in Ministry*, 121-32.

Chapter 5

1. Collins, *Good to Great*, 44.

Chapter 7

1. John Maxwell, Injoy Life Club audiocassette—"What Every Staff Member Wants from Their Pastor" (Atlanta: Injoy, 1999), Year 15-4.

Chapter 8

1. The pastors in order of reference include Pastor Mark Fuller of Crossroads Church of the Nazarene, Chandler, Ariz.; Dr. J. K. Warrick of Olathe College Church of the Nazarene, Kans.; Dr. Tim Stearman of Denver First Church of the Nazarene; Dr. Larry Leonard of Lakeland Highland Park Church of the Nazarene, Fla.; and Dr. Mel McCullough of Bethany First Church of the Nazarene, Okla.

Chapter 9

1. Gary Sivewright, letter written from Mount Vernon, Ohio, March 15, 2002.
2. Helmut Thielicke, *The Waiting Father* (New York: Harper and Row, 1959), 143.